Issues on Gender and Diversity in Management

Ralph Ocon

UNIVERSITY PRESS OF AMERICA,® INC.
Lanham • Boulder • New York • Toronto • Oxford

Copyright © 2006 by
University Press of America,® Inc.
4501 Forbes Boulevard
Suite 200
Lanham, Maryland 20706
UPA Acquisitions Department (301) 459-3366

PO Box 317
Oxford
OX2 9RU, UK

Library of Congress Control Number: 2006929004
ISBN-13: 978-0-7618-3543-1 (paperback : alk. paper)
ISBN-10: 0-7618-3543-1 (paperback : alk. paper)

Contents

Preface   v

Acknowledgments   xi

Introduction   xiii

1   Introduction to Diversity in the Workplace   1

2   Equal Employment Opportunity and Affirmative Action   10

3   Stereotyping, Prejudice, and Discrimination   23

4   Women in the Workplace   36

5   Cultural Values and Communication   46

6   Disabilities and the Workplace   58

7   Recruiting for a Diverse Workforce   67

8   New Generations in the Workplace   77

9   Resolving Diversity Related Disputes   87

10 Multicultural Leadership and Teambuilding   95

11 Sexual Orientation and the Workplace   105

12 Developing a Diversity Program   114

Glossary   129

References   135

About the Author   137

Preface

IMPORTANCE OF DIVERSITY EDUCATION

The author's diversity related research, and experience as an equal employment opportunity officer, teacher and trainer for the university and industry have made him aware of the need for diversity education. The omnipresent effects of globalization have increased the frequency of interaction and degree of interdependence between nations and diverse people forcing American society and the business community to have to deal with diversity issues. The American workplace confronting today's supervisor is much different from the workplace of 40 years ago. Globalization and workforce diversity have influenced the way organizations manage their human resources. Therefore, success for American businesses is contingent on the abilities of supervisors to understand and work with people from diverse backgrounds and cultures on an organizational, national and international level. As the future leaders of business organizations and the global community, students will need to learn how to effectively interact and manage people who are different or perceived to be different.

Acknowledging the future leadership roles of students, many university curricula are emphasizing the importance of diversity education to help students develop their leadership skills. As potential leaders, students will have a tremendous impact on upcoming events that will affect everyone everywhere. Consequently, diversity education is one of the key types of training students in every academic major must receive if they are going to be effective leaders. Not only is diversity education important for students, it's also important for anyone currently employed or looking for employment.

BENEFITS OF DIVERSITY EDUCATION

Although diversity presents certain concerns that American society and the business community must learn to deal with, it also offers the potential for enormous benefits and opportunities. Table 0.1 lists some of the major benefits American businesses can derive from diversity education.

Table 0.1:   Major Benefits to American Businesses from Diversity Education

- Creates acceptance of people as they are without regard to race, culture, gender or other differentiating characteristics
- Promotes social responsibility and ethical behavior by encouraging fair and equitable treatment for everyone
- Promotes communication and relationship development among diverse employees
- Recognition of diversity as a legitimate business issue and part of strategic planning
- Improves teambuilding and the ability to work with diverse employees
- Promotes a management style that is conducive with a diverse workforce
- Establishes employee pride associated with ethnic identity and cultural heritage
- Promotes individualism
- Avoids or limits employment discrimination complaints and lawsuits
- Recognition that different thinking styles can improve decision-making and problem-solving
- Recognition that different thinking styles can promote creative and innovative thinking
- Recognition of diversity as a business resource or advantage which can be used to effectively compete in the global economy
- Promotes proactive behavior by creating awareness of diversity issues and concerns

ISSUES BASED LEARNING

Developing multicultural leadership skills is the type of training supervisors and future leaders must receive to be effective leaders. Until recently the training and education on how to manage diversity have often been overlooked or not adequately covered in most leadership/supervisory training programs and management books, and therefore, most management courses.

Consequently, the author has developed an issues based learning approach as an effective way to teach diversity management. Based on the author's research and experience in diversity, twelve critical diversity issues have been identified and used as the principal means for teaching diversity management. By discussing these issues, students are able to gain awareness and understanding of the diversity concerns which will enable them to develop effective multicultural leadership skills. Under each issue are several articles related to that issue that facilitate the learning of diversity management. Because the diversity issues identified and developed by the author are interesting, relevant and contemporary, students have responded well to this teaching approach.

ORIGINS OF ISSUES BASED LEARNING

Using issues, instead of chapters, is an alternative and effective approach for introducing and discussing the topics of diversity management. The issues identified provide instructors with more teaching flexibility than do chapters. The author originally developed the idea for teaching diversity management using issues based learning from his success in using this approach to teach other types of courses. For example, in the past, the author used an issues based learning approach to teach various courses in economics and law. Based on the author's experience and success in helping students understand analytical and multifaceted subjects such as economics and law, he employed the issues based approach when providing diversity training workshops for the university and industry. Currently, the author uses an issue based learning approach to teach diversity management with both in-class and online courses.

The issues based approach allows instructors to introduce diversity issues in a nonpartisan and non-confrontational manner and provides students with the opportunity to analyze their perceptions about diversity and the management of diversity. The issues are also adaptable to the experience and expertise of the instructor. Both experienced and less experienced instructors of diversity management can effectively present the diversity issues and engage in either a detailed or general discussion of selected issues. Also, the issues based approach allows instructors the opportunity to gradually develop their expertise in diversity management. Because the teaching of diversity management often involves controversial subject matter and generates strong emotions, some instructors might initially be reluctant to use traditional teaching methods, such as lecturing or assigning chapters to read. However, an issues based learning approach allows for the discussion of multifaceted, controversial and emotional diversity topics to develop naturally, where different viewpoints surrounding the issues can be exchanged in a non-threatening manner.

BENEFITS OF ISSUES BASED LEARNING

From the perspective of instructors and students, issues provide an alternative and interesting approach for teaching and learning about diversity management.

Based on the author's research and over twenty years of teaching experience, students enjoy reading and discussing issues, rather than relying on the traditional approach of assigning chapters to read or listening to lectures on diversity management. Table 0.2 lists some of the major reasons students like the issues based learning approach. By using the twelve critical diversity issues, "Issues On Gender And Diversity In Management" exposes students to a variety of diversity related concerns that must be understood for the effective management of diversity and development of multicultural leadership skills.

Table 0.2:   Reasons Students Like Issues Based Learning

- Student centered
- Interactive learning method
- Creates awareness of different viewpoints
- Can engage in detailed/general discussions
- Encourages students to use different thinking skills
- Embraces outcome based learning
- An alternative and fun way to learn
- A natural and interesting way to learn
- Challenges the beliefs of students
- Complements other teaching methods and activities
- Expands the disciplinary breadth and depth of the subject
- Subject expertise is not required for class discussions
- A subtle or indirect way to raise the awareness of controversial diversity issues

ORIGIN OF THE TWELVE CRITICAL DIVERSITY ISSUES

During the author's twelve years as a university Equal Employment Opportunity Officer, he investigated and resolved over one hundred complaints of harassment and discrimination filed with his office by faculty, staff, students and people in the community. Over the years in dealing with these complaints, the author identified recurring issues and discovered that the majority of complaints could have been avoided or more easily resolved had the parties involved had some training and understanding of basic diversity issues.

As a consultant and trainer for local industry, the author trained thousands of employees in diversity management using the issues based learning approach. Also, because most of the available diversity management books did not adequately identify all the critical diversity issues involved in the workplace, the issues based learning approach using the twelve critical issues for teaching diversity management was developed. Consequently, based on the author's equal employment opportunity and industry training experience, and research of diversity management, the twelve critical issues were developed as a proactive approach for diversity management.

ISSUES AND ARTICLES

"Issues On Gender And Diversity In Management" contains forty diversity management articles written by the author which promote the understanding of the twelve critical issues. These articles reflect the diversity concerns researched and experienced by the author as an Equal Employment Opportunity Officer and industry consultant/trainer. The book is written to meet the needs of students in courses such as diversity management, human relations for supervisors, general management, leadership development, ethnic studies and communications. Also, the diversity issues and articles can be introduced at any point during the study of a related management topic.

The twelve diversity issues identified in the book are relevant, contemporary and controversial. Although each issue can be a self-contained learning module, instructors have the opportunity to supplement class discussions with other learning methods. Under each issue are several articles related to that issue. Review questions and learning activities are available at the end of each issue to facilitate further discussion and understanding. Also, a glossary is provided to define, and further promote the understanding of diversity related terms and concepts.

With two exceptions, the order for introducing and discussing the twelve diversity issues is not important. It is recommended that Issue 1 be examined first because it provides an effective way to introduce the subject of diversity and managing diversity. Issue 12 is recommended to be examined last since it concludes the subject of managing diversity by identifying the importance of organizational change and the major components of a diversity program. Issues 2–11 can be discussed in any order without creating any disruption or confusion in the subject matter.

THE TWELVE CRITICAL DIVERSITY ISSUES

Issue 1: Introduction To Diversity In The Workplace: introduces the topic of diversity, managing diversity and its importance for American businesses.

Issue 2: Equal Employment Opportunity & Affirmative Action: examines the equal employment opportunity laws and the controversial issue of affirmative action, including arguments for and against it.

Issue 3: Stereotyping, Prejudice And Discrimination: looks at stereotyping, prejudice and discrimination in the workplace, and ways to deal with these concerns.

Issue 4: Women In The Workplace: identifies the workplace issues confronting women employees and supervisors, and how to deal with those concerns.

Issue 5: Cultural Values And Communication: focuses on cultural values and intercultural communication, and how they can influence relationships in the workplace.

Issue 6: Disabilities And The Workplace: deals with employees with disabilities and how supervisors can effectively manage them.

Issue 7: Recruiting For A Diverse Workforce: focuses on the hiring process and on how to effectively recruit diversity.

Issue 8: New Generations In The Workplace: discusses the need for continuous education and introduces the newest generations of employees, Generation X and Generation Y.

Issue 9: Resolving Diversity Related Disputes: deals with workplace conflicts and how to manage diversity related disputes.

Issue 10: Multicultural Leadership And Teambuilding: focuses on how to develop the skills required for multicultural leadership and teambuilding.

Issue 11: Sexual Orientation And The Workplace: examines the controversial issue of sexual orientation and how to deal with the concerns of gay and lesbian employees.

Issue 12: Developing A Diversity Program: identifies the major components of a diversity program and how organizations can successfully implement such a program.

Acknowledgments

Writing this book on diversity management has been a major goal the author has been pursuing for several years. Although the book is being published this year, drafts of the book have been used in the author's diversity management course for several years. The book represents a compilation of the author's diversity management research, and experiences as a university Equal Employment Opportunity Officer and industry consultant/trainer.

Having achieved this goal, the author would like to take this opportunity to express his thanks and appreciation. First, the author would like to thank Professor Carl F. Jenks for his continuous support and mentorship throughout the author's career at Purdue University Calumet.

In addition to Professor Jenks, the author would like to express his gratitude to the Dean of the School of Technology, Dennis P. Korchek, for his support. Also, thanks to the faculty and staff of the Manufacturing Engineering Technologies and Supervision (METS) Department for their support, especially Professor Lash B. Mapa, Computer Aided Design Coordinator, David McLees, and OLS secretary, Diane Moody. Additionally, the Purdue University Calumet students who have taken the author's diversity management course deserve recognition for their feedback on the initial drafts of the book, with special thanks to Opal B. McFarlane. Finally, the author would like to express his appreciation for the unremitting encouragement, support, and guidance provided by the author's parents, Jesus and Ruby Ocon.

Introduction

GLOBALIZATION

Today, the world is more dynamic, complex, and diverse than what it was ten years ago and this trend will continue into the future. As the globalization process continues, the degree of interaction and interdependence between nations and diverse people will also increase, creating the need for greater understanding and cooperation for global harmony and prosperity to be realized. The ability to establish effective relationships with diverse people throughout the world has become increasing important for American society and the world in general.

The omnipresent effects of globalization will force every person, business and nation to have to deal with diversity issues. Therefore, success in any endeavor, including the management of human resources, will be contingent on the ability to understand diversity and get along with diverse people. Over the last several decades much progress has been made in the areas of egalitarianism, civil rights, civility and establishing positive relationships between diverse people, resulting in the development of laws, and business policies, practices and training designed to eliminate prejudice, harassment and discrimination in the workplace.

HISTORICAL FEAR OF DIVERSITY

Unfortunately, throughout history the misunderstanding and fear about people who are perceived to be different have been a major source of controversy and an obstacle to harmony in American society and the global community. History cites numerous examples of how ignorance or the lack of understanding of diversity has resulted in stereotyping, prejudice and inappropriate behavior. In the workplace, stereotyping, prejudice and discrimination resulting from the misunderstanding about employees who are considered to be "different" can, not only undermine relationships but, have a negative impact on organizational performance, morale and the ability to compete in the global economy. Research and experience conclude that diversity education and the development of multicultural leadership skills are essential for effectively managing a diverse workforce.

In the wake of 9-11 and other recent events, both domestic and foreign, emphasis has been placed on ways to reduce the threat of terrorism and ensure national/homeland security. Unfortunately, these events have also perpetuated and even escalated the fear of diversity, especially people from other cultures, and made some Americans so obsessed about terrorism and national security that they have forgotten about the benefits of diversity. In fact, some Americans have the false belief that promoting national security and establishing positive relationships with people from different cultural groups are mutually exclusive endeavors. It's imperative that American businesses do not forego the benefits of diversity due to stereotypes and prejudice based on the misunderstanding about people from other cultures.

American businesses must exercise care to not undermine the decades of advances made in workforce diversity because of fears about people from other cultures. Left unchecked, this fear can escalate and not only impede further development in the area of diversity and intercultural relationships, but reverse much of the progress made, resulting in greater misunderstanding, fear, prejudice and discrimination against diverse people in the workplace, American society and the global community.

DIVERSITY EDUCATION AND THE BUSINESS COMMUNITY

As is true with most concerns, the solution for overcoming the misunderstanding and fear associated with diversity and promoting relationship development lies with diversity education. Such education can provide the knowledge necessary to create mutual understanding and respect between diverse people.

In the forthcoming years, students and young adults will make decisions and take actions, either positive or negative, that will affect future events for everyone everywhere. As the future leaders, problem-solvers and policy-makers of business organizations and the global society in general, young adults will need to understand diversity and the benefits of interacting with diverse people. Although improving relationships between people, especially diverse people, is a complex undertaking, the long term effects from such an endeavor will be favorable for everyone.

The American business community has a unique opportunity to positively influence relationships among diverse people on an organizational, national and global scale. At the same time, corporate America can fulfill its social responsibility to treat everyone in an ethical and equitable manner, and act in ways that are consistent with being a role model for American society and the global community. Through globalization, American companies will continue to be exposed to people from different cultures and as a result, have the opportunity to promote mutual understanding and respect. With its policies and practices, the American business community can improve its global image and have a positive influence on intercultural relationships throughout the world.

Consequently, at a time when the U.S. is recognized as a military and economic superpower, with the help of the business community, it has the opportunity to play a pivotal role in promoting global harmony and achieving recognition as an equalitarian superpower.

Through diversity education, managers and employees of American companies can learn how to effectively interact with diversity, both in the U.S. and abroad. Such education can promote civility, and the mutual understanding and respect necessary for the effective management of diversity. The effects of education will not only benefit U.S. businesses as they pursue globalization, but the global community in general. In the long term, diversity education can improve relationships within organizations and between the U.S. and other cultures of the world while simultaneously promoting the advantages of diversity. Given the interdependent nature of the global community, in time, diverse people may come to realize that they have more in common with each other than differences and by working together everyone can benefit.

As is true with many of the challenges confronting American society and the workplace, diversity issues are concerns that are confronting the rest of the world. Therefore, diversity will continue to be a worldwide concern for society, government, business and academia. As the world becomes smaller and interaction between diverse people increases, learning how to effectively interact with people who are different, including the management of a diverse workforce, will remain as major issues for global discussion.

Issue One

Introduction to Diversity in the Workplace

"Globalization and workforce diversity require a new management approach"

Issue One highlights the importance of diversity and managing diversity. Traditionally, how diversity was treated or managed was not given much consideration because the management of diversity was primarily viewed from an ethical or moral standpoint. Also, the process of assimilation was assumed to be the natural and most effective approach for dealing with diversity. However, globalization and the changing demographics of the workforce have made the management of diversity a legitimate business concern with implications for organizational survival and success.

The new philosophy on how to deal with diverse people contradicts a popular approach for developing relationships. Treating people the way they like to be treated focuses on the fact that everyone is an individual, with unique personalities and specific needs. For successful leadership, supervisors must take the time to get to know their employees instead of relying on traditional stereotypes about people based on culture, ethnicity or appearance.

MANAGING DIVERSITY IN THE WORKPLACE

The American workforce has experienced dramatic changes in its composition over the last several decades. For example, during the 1990s, over 85% of employees who entered the U.S. labor force were composed of women, minorities and immigrants, with roughly 45% of this net addition being minorities and immigrants, and almost two-thirds being women. As the workforce continues to diversify, supervisors are going to be challenged on how to manage and work with diversity. Managing and working with people who look,

1

think or act different can be difficult and uncomfortable for some of us. This is especially true when there is a lack information or experience in dealing with diversity. Consequently, we may not know what to say or how to behave around people who are "different" or perceived to be different.

In today's workplace, employees have various characteristics or differences that may appear to be obvious during an initial encounter. At the same time, other characteristics or differences may not become known until later in the relationship. Examples of employee characteristics that are readily apparent include differences in gender, age, and race. Characteristics that may not be obvious during an initial encounter include differences in sexual orientation, lifestyles, certain mental or physical limitations, education, seniority within an organization, geographic origins, goals, ambitions, attitudes and values. This mixture of people with various backgrounds, experiences and characteristics, both obvious and obscure, is referred to as "diversity."

The greater the number of employee differences that exist within an organization, the greater the organizational diversity that exist. Consequently, some organizations are more diverse than others. At the same time, the greater the diversity that exist within an organization, the greater the potential for people related problems to develop. Alternatively, a high degree of employee diversity presents more opportunities for those organizations to capitalize on the benefits that diversity can provide.

Although diversity has always been a prominent part of American culture, only within the last three decades has concern grown over how to effectively manage our diverse workforce. The traditional management philosophies in most organizations on how to deal with diverse employees were to either ignore differences or promote assimilation. Until recently, assimilation was thought to be the best approach for managing diversity and thereby became the chosen approach for most organizations. Through assimilation, organizations encouraged employees to conform to a certain stereotype of how the "ideal" employee should look and behave. Generally, this stereotype was based on the values, beliefs and traditions of white, heterosexual, non-disabled, males. Ultimately, this stereotype influenced decision-making and behavior about employees within the typical organization and pressured them to, either conform to it or find employment elsewhere.

Based on research and experience, most diversity experts agree that treating all employees as if they were the same or trying to force them to become the same is not an effective way to manage a diverse workforce. Instead, most experts believe that organizations need to value and utilize employee differences if they are to successfully compete in the global economy. Consequently, rather than eliminating or trying to conceal differences among employees, organizations need to recognize and value employee differences.

Valuing diversity makes economic sense because an organization's most valuable asset is its employees. The key to being competitive in a global economy is to develop and utilize the talents and abilities of every employee, regardless of their culture or background. Diversity is a key characteristic that distinguishes American culture from that of other nations. No other nation in the world has the degree of diversity that the U.S. has. Diversity is what makes the U.S. culture unique and if properly managed, can provide a competitive advantage for American businesses. Therefore, employers need to capitalize on this economic advantage in order to survive and successfully compete with companies in other nations.

To effectively manage a diverse workforce, American employers need to be proactive and initiate changes that reflect the new reality. The term used to identify the type of change organizations need to implement in order to deal effectively with diversity is often referred to as "managing diversity." Managing diversity refers to a change process that will impact the entire organization by promoting inclusiveness within the organization. By creating an inclusive workplace, the needs of the employees and management can be simultaneously promoted and satisfied. Managing diversity requires organizations to develop policies and practices that benefit everyone, regardless of their differences and ensures that all employees will have the opportunities to develop their careers and advance within the organization. Because managing diversity benefits all employees, the change process should encounter little resistance if it is properly implemented.

Management must recognize that diversity in the workplace is not a temporary fad, but a long term trend that is continuing to grow. Different types of diversity are being recognized and emerging everyday, from cultural and generational diversity to individual diversity. At the same time, the globalization process, where people throughout the world are interacting with each other on a daily basis, has made diversity an international concern. Consequently, diversity is going to remain a continual management concern and require that supervisors learn how to effectively manage it.

WHY "MANAGING DIVERSITY" IS IMPORTANT

An important ingredient for the success of every organization is to be proactive and initiate change before major problems develop. "Managing diversity" is a proactive organizational change process designed to create an inclusive work environment which can satisfy the needs of management and the employees. In the past, assimilation was thought to be the best approach for dealing with a diverse workforce. Whereas the focus of assimilation was to change the employee from what he/she was and into a fictional and stereo-type ideal of what some thought an employee should be, managing diversity is designed to change the organizational culture into one that promotes diversity. Most diversity experts agree that it is easier and more effective to change the organizational culture than to try and change who a person is.

At the same time, managing diversity has become a legitimate business concern that is economically required for organizational survival and success.

Why Managing Diversity Is Necessary

Global Economy

Globalization has had a major impact on how companies compete and manage their resources. American businesses are competing against those of other nations in an international marketplace comprised of over 6 billion potential customers and clients. Satisfying the needs of the global economy will require an understanding of different cultures. Therefore, American companies who have diverse employees will be better able to relate, understand and interact with consumers of other cultures and nations.

Because of the degree of diversity that exists in the U.S workforce, American companies which properly manage diversity can have a competitive advantage over companies in other nations which have relatively homogenous workforces. Also, by having the opportunity to learn about the cultures of their employees, supervisors and employees in American organizations can simultaneously learn about the cultures and needs of their customers and clients located in different parts of the world. Consequently, American companies must capitalize on the diversity of their employees and make business decisions that reflect international perspectives.

Labor Force Composition

The composition of the America labor force has undergone dramatic changes, especially within the last 40 years. For example, there are more women, minorities, older workers, workers with disabilities, workers from different generations and other types of diversity in the American workforce. As a result, organizations cannot rely on past leadership methods and techniques for managing their diverse human resources, but instead, need techniques that are conducive with the new reality. Multicultural, multigenerational or other types of diversity related leadership skills are necessary for the effective supervision of a diverse workforce.

Competition for Labor

There is a critical shortage of the skilled labor necessary to provide the types and quantity of goods and services needed to satisfy the over 6 billion consumers in the global economy. Recognizing this shortage, American companies must compete, not only with each other for the limited supply of skilled labor, but must also compete with companies in other nations. No organization is so successful that it can afford to overlook any qualified and talented source of potential employees. Therefore, managing diversity will enable American companies to recruit and retain the best qualified employees and in the process help to ensure organizational success.

New Worker Attitude

Today, the diverse employees in the American workforce, especially younger employees, are not willing to assimilate to traditional employee stereotypes by giving up their ethnic identity and cultural heritage. Nor are they willing to accept a workplace that does not satisfy their personal and professional needs. Employees want to be recognized and valued for their individuality. Consequently, for recruitment and retention purposes, organizations will need to create "diversity friendly" workplaces where supervisors view and treat each employee as an individual.

Moral and Ethical Reasons

From a moral and ethical standpoint, supervisors should not view or treat their employees based on race, ethnicity, gender or other subjective and non-job related factors. At the same time, it is unfair for supervisors to use subjective and non-job related criteria to evaluate employee performance and make employment decisions. Instead, from a moral and ethical standpoint, supervisors should view and treat their employees as individuals and make employment decisions based on objective and job related criteria.

Legal Reasons

From a legal standpoint, managing diversity can help to ensure that supervisors treat and evaluate each employee as an individual. Equal employment opportunity laws, such as Title VII of the 1964 Civil Rights Act, require that supervisors evaluate their employees and base employment decisions on objective and job related criteria. Managing diversity requires organizations to design proactive policies to prevent harassment, discrimination and other types of illegal and unfair behavior in the workplace. This is especially important considering the fact that employees who belong to protected groups comprise over 70 percent of the U.S. workforce.

Improved Decision-Making

A diversity of thinking styles can promote new ideas and thereby improve organizational decision making and problem solving. For survival and success in the global economy, organizations need to develop and implement creative and innovative ideas. Interaction between employees from diverse cultures, backgrounds and experiences can result in positive synergies when different perspectives and viewpoints are discussed and developed. Therefore, these interactions can improve the quality of decision making and problem solving.

Economic Resource

Managing diversity is about recognizing and utilizing the strengths of a diverse workforce. The U.S. has more diversity, both in quality and quantity, than any other country of the world. Unfortunately, for much of American's history, diversity was often viewed as something negative and a major source of problems in society and the workplace. Today, most diversity experts agree that American's diversity can become a business asset and competitive advantage if properly managed.

Awareness of Diversity Issues

Awareness of diversity issues can help American organizations to become proactive and prevent problems before they occur. The global economy and workforce diversity present new challenges for employers and supervisors. Managing diversity promotes an awareness of current and future diversity issues and the development of future oriented strategies for dealing with those issues. A proactive management approach provides organizations with more alternatives for dealing with different situations than does a reactive management approach.

It's taken a while, but more and more organizations are beginning to realize and capitalize on the benefits associated with a diverse workforce.

THE GOLDEN RULE FOR THE NEW MILLENNIUM

Throughout history, different philosophies have emerged over how to effectively interact with people. In the workplace, the relationships that are established between the employees and the supervisor influence the various functions of an organization. One of the more popular approaches for developing effective interpersonal relationships has been to follow the Golden Rule, "do onto others as you would have others do onto you." In other words, we should treat others as we would like to be treated. At first glance the Golden Rule may appear to make practical sense, easy to apply and the solution for relationship development. However, as is true with most generalities about people and human behavior this rule stereotypes people and may even impede relationship development. Especially with today's diverse workforce, the Golden Rule is not a complete or accurate guide on how to effectively deal with people. Unfortunately, too many supervisors believe in this one size fits all approach to human relations and automatically rely on it when interacting with employees.

The Golden Rule is based on the "Me Principle," which is the belief that everyone is the same or thinks the same as everyone else. Unfortunately, when we believe that everyone is the same, we assume everyone wants to be treated the same way. Therefore, the Golden Rule stereotypes people and is based on the assumption that everyone is basically alike, having the same needs, values, beliefs and interests. It does not take into account that each person is different from every other person or that people may want to feel special and recognized as individuals. If we treat people the way we like to be treated, then we are not treating them the way they want to be treated. As a result, we are not recognizing people as individuals and thus, not satisfying their personal needs.

The Golden Rule may be a useful guide to follow when interacting with someone we just met. For example, during an initial encounter with someone, we rely on stereotypes and assumptions since we don't have much information about a person. Unfortunately, too many of us continue to rely on the Golden Rule indefinitely, without taking the time or making the effort to know and understand one another. Therefore, we should remember that a behavioral guide resulting in early relationship success may end up undermining later success.

Traditional supervisory training programs often emphasized the Golden Rule and encouraged supervisors to view and treat all employees the same. Differences among employees were supposed to be ignored and thought to be divisive factors in the workplace. The Golden Rule allowed supervisors the luxury of not having to interact with their employees, spend time with them or get to know and understand them in order to be effective. Consequently, in one sense this rule made the supervisor's job easy since it provided a seemingly simple solution to the management of employees and relationship development.

However, the short term consequence of this approach in the workplace was at best, average employee performance and moderate job satisfaction. In the long term, the Golden Rule discouraged relationship development and ignored potential human relations problems because supervisors failed to take the time or make the effort to understand their employees.

Competition in the global economy will not allow average performing organizations to continue to survive. Therefore, it's imperative for supervisors to develop skills that will enhance their managerial capabilities, since the success of an organization is directly related to the quality of supervision. Today, we know that treating all employees the same or trying to force them to become the same is not an effective way to interact with people or manage diversity.

In the new millennium, effective interpersonal relationships require that supervisors follow a revised or New Golden Rule, "do onto others as they would do onto to themselves." In other words, "we should treat others as they would like to be treated." This new rule reflects the essence of human individuality or the fact that everyone is different from everyone else. It focuses on treating people as individuals by taking the time to learn how each person wants to be treated. Although we have certain basic needs that require fulfillment, how each person satisfies those needs differs from one person to another. For example, we all have the need for food and clothing, but each person satisfies their food and clothing needs in different ways. If we consider the degree of diversity throughout the world and the variety of food and clothing options available, it's easy to understand the rationale underlying the New Golden Rule.

Today, diversity training programs need to encourage supervisors to recognize and utilize individual differences in order to obtain the benefits of a diverse workforce. Organizations can achieve improved performance and job satisfaction if employees are recognize, valued and treated as individuals, rather than stereotyped and treated the same. By exercising flexible leadership and taking the time to know their employees, supervisors can learn how each employee wants to be treated.

As is true when learning any skill, developing effective "people skills" is not always easy. Supervisors need to understand that promoting relationships is an on-going process which requires time, patience and effort. Although people should be treated as equals, they should not be treated the same. The New Golden Rule is a progressive approach for developing effective interpersonal relationships that is not only wanted by employees, but needed by American organizations.

REVIEW QUESTIONS

1. The term "Diversity" includes non-minority males.
2. When dealing with people from other cultures, we should treat them the way we like to be treated.
3. "Managing Diversity" is an organizational change process.
4. Today, the average employee in the U.S. labor force is younger compared with previous generations of employees.
5. The traditional approach used by American companies for dealing with diversity was assimilation.
6. Today, the majority of jobs in the U.S. are in the manufacturing sector of the economy.
7. A diverse workforce is an economic resource.
8. All employees will benefit from "Managing Diversity."
9. What is the type of unemployment that is caused by changes in technology and automation?
10. The U.S. represents approximately 10 percent of the world's population.

LEARNING ACTIVITIES

1. Divide the class into teams and have each team discuss what can be learned from a given minority or cultural group.
2. Assign students or teams of students to research and discuss the historical backgrounds of different minority or cultural groups.

Issue Two

Equal Employment Opportunity and Affirmative Action

"Legal issues have become a major fact of business life"

Issue Two focuses on the major diversity related laws often referred to as equal employment opportunity, and the controversial and emotional issue of affirmative action. Recognition of the purpose and the difference between equal employment opportunity and affirmative action are important for understanding how to manage diversity. Awareness of the basic principles of law can reduce the anxiety and uncertainty supervisors sometimes experience when managing diversity.

Legal issues have become a major component of the supervisor's job, especially those laws that are directly related to diversity. Given the fact that 70 percent of all employees in the American workforce are members of protected groups, supervisors must exercise care when taking actions or making employment decisions in order to avoid diversity related lawsuits.

AFFIRMATIVE ACTION DOES NOT MEAN EQUAL EMPLOYMENT OPPORTUNITY

The topic of diversity is filled with a number of distinctive and sometimes confusing terms and concepts which need to be accurately defined and described to promote the understanding of diversity management. For example, one of the areas of confusion has to do with the misunderstanding between equal employment opportunity (EEO) and affirmative action (AA). These two terms are often thought of as having the same meaning and are therefore incorrectly used interchangeably. Adding to the confusion is the fact that in most organizations there is one person who may be referred to as an equal employment opportunity officer, affirmative action officer or diversity specialist and has direct responsibility for administering diversity related concerns. In reality, there is a great deal of difference between these two terms.

Equal Employment Opportunity

Equal employment opportunity is a legal duty and generally refers to the three principal federal anti-discrimination laws which regulate most aspects of the employment relationship. Most employers are required to follow the three laws underlying equal employment opportunity. These three laws are Title VII of the 1964 Civil Rights Act, the Age Discrimination in Employment Act of 1967 and the Americans With Disabilities Act of 1990. Equal employment opportunity prohibits discrimination in employment based on a job applicant's or employee's race, color, religion, national origin, gender, disability or age. In other words, when making employment decisions, employers and supervisors are prohibited from considering any of the above mentioned characteristics. Equal employment opportunity applies to virtually every aspect of employment, including recruiting, hiring, wages, training, promotion, benefits, discipline, layoff, termination and retirement.

Affirmative Action

Although equal employment opportunity is the general rule of law in employment decision-making, the exception to this rule is affirmative action. Affirmative action allows preferential treatment under specific circumstances based on a job applicant's race or gender when making hiring and/or promotion decisions. If certain conditions are met, affirmative action allows an employer to consider an applicant's race or gender when deciding whether to hire or promote that person. In order words, in addition to evaluating an applicant's job related qualifications for a position, affirmative action allows the employer to consider the applicant's race or gender as a "plus" factor when deciding who should be hired. How much consideration is given to an applicant's race or gender when making hiring decisions is left to the discretion of each employer? Whereas, equal employment opportunity applies to most aspects of employment decision-making, affirmative action only applies to recruiting, hiring and promotion.

Because equal employment opportunity is the law, virtually all employers have a legal duty to follow it. The same is not true for affirmative action. Affirmative action is a proactive employment initiative designed to increase the number of women and minorities in the workforce.

Most affirmative action programs are voluntarily undertaken by employers and basically represent a promise or commitment by an employer to actively recruit, hire and promote qualified women, minorities, persons with disabilities and Vietnam Era veterans. Also, affirmative action is only required of the government and private employers with contracts (government contractors) to perform services or supply products to the federal government. In limited situations, affirmative action may be legally required or ordered by a judge if an employer is found guilty of past employment discrimination.

Some believe affirmative action mandates hiring "quotas." If quotas were legal, they would require that a fixed number or percentage of women or minorities be hired by a given employer. However, quotas are generally illegal and if they are used by employers, quotas can result in lawsuits of reverse discrimination by non-minority males. What affirmative action does allow is hiring "goals," which are distinctly different from quotas. Goals require the employer to exercise good faith efforts to recruit, hire and promote qualified women and minorities if an underutilization of women or minorities exist in certain job categories in an employer's workforce. At the same time, goals allow the employer to hire the most qualified person for a job, whether that person is a woman, minority or non-minority male even if an underutilization exists in an employer's workforce.

When originally developed, affirmative action was thought to be a short term policy and expected to continue only as long as an underutilization of women and minorities existed in the workforce. On the other hand, equal employment opportunity is considered to be a long term employment policy and expected to continue indefinitely.

It's important for supervisors and employees to understand the difference between these two terms. Although affirmative action and equal employment opportunity have different meanings, both terms are related because they represent major components of diversity management and are attempting to promote employment opportunities for all qualified individuals. Therefore, awareness of the meanings and purpose of these terms can help to promote understanding and ensure that equal employment opportunity and affirmative action are being properly used.

PROTECTED GROUPS AND THE LAW

There are legal aspects and consequences associated with virtually every employment decision, especially when diversity related concerns or issues are involved. Therefore, understanding the basic laws that govern the employment relationship is critical for effectively managing a diverse workforce.

Managing diversity can be particularly difficult when management decisions or actions involve employees who are members of protected groups. A specific set of employment laws, the antidiscrimination laws, create the potential for additional liability to result if complaints and lawsuits of discrimination are filed. Therefore, greater care must be exercised when dealing with employees who belong to protected groups.

Protected groups refer to employees who possess certain characteristics or traits that the law has determined should be given a protected legal status. At the federal level, these legally protected characteristics or traits are gender, race, color, national origin, religion, disability and age. The following three principal federal laws prohibit employers and supervisors from making any employment decisions or taking any actions based on the above listed characteristics.

- Title VII of the 1964 Civil Rights Act (Title VII)
- Age Discrimination in Employment Act of 1967 (ADEA)
- Americans With Disabilities Act of 1990 (ADA)

These three laws are often referred to as equal employment opportunity laws, fair employment laws, diversity laws or the anti-discrimination laws, and are designed to protect women, minorities, people 40 or over in age, and people who have disabilities from employment discrimination. Contrary to what some may believe, the anti-discrimination laws do not prohibit all employment discrimination, only certain types of discrimination. For example, it is legal if an employer bases an employment decision on an applicant's education, experience, skills and other job related considerations. Therefore, when deciding who to hire or promote, an employer can consider an applicant's work history, but not their race, can consider the work related opinions of an applicant's previous employers, but not the subjective and non-job related opinions about the applicant.

Employees who are dissatisfied with management decisions or actions can file complaints of discrimination with governmental agencies, such as the Equal Employment Opportunity Commission, or lawsuits in state and federal courts. It is important for employers and supervisors to understand their legal responsibilities and obligations imposed by these laws in order to recognize the legal issues and potential consequences involved when making decisions or taking actions. Consequently, employers cannot use "ignorance of the law" as a defense to avoid liability when laws are violated.

By understanding these three federal antidiscrimination laws, employers and supervisors can significantly improve their knowledge and expertise about diversity issues in general, and avoid most legal problems involving employees who are members of protected groups. For example, understanding these three laws can help supervisors avoid legal problems when dealing with the following diversity issues.

Affirmative Action

Because affirmative action is a controversial and emotional issue, it has the potential for misunderstanding, complaints and lawsuits. For those organizations that have affirmative action programs, Title VII requires that these programs follow specific legal requirements in order to avoid lawsuits by non-minority males for reverse discrimination.

Stereotyping and Prejudice

Despite the progress that has been made in educating supervisors and employees about the benefits of a diverse workforce, negative stereotyping and prejudice still exist. Understanding Title VII can motivate supervisors and employees to analyze and change their thinking and attitudes about diverse employees and thereby avoid discriminatory behaviors.

Women in the Workplace

Women comprise over 47 percent of the U.S. workforce, therefore employers and supervisors need to be aware of the legal issues related to the management of women employees. Liability resulting from complaints of sexual harassment and sex discrimination can be avoided if employers and supervisors have a general understanding of Title VII.

Cultural Values

Different cultural values create the potential for misunderstanding and complaints. Because a person's culture has a major impact on values, beliefs and behaviors, the relevant diversity laws need to be considered when managing people. Understanding Title VII can reduce liability resulting from complaints of race, national origin and religion discrimination.

Language

Over 26 percent of the U.S. labor force consists of minorities and immigrants, many of who speak English as a second language. Confusion concerning an employer's right to establish workplace rules on foreign accents and language can be avoided if there is an understanding of the relevant laws. Therefore, to avoid complaints and lawsuits based on national origin harassment and discrimination, employers and supervisors need to be aware of Title VII.

Disabilities

There are over 54 million people in the U.S. who have protected disabilities. Many employers and supervisors are uncertain about what disabilities are protected or how to supervise and interact with applicants or employees with disabilities. To avoid liability for discrimination based on disabilities, employers and supervisors need to have an awareness of the ADA.

Hiring and Promotion

Filling job vacancies can create the potential for complaints and lawsuits by both job applicants and current employees. Job descriptions, job specifications, interviews and testing can play a major role in selecting the best qualified person. Awareness of the legal requirements imposed on employers and supervisors by Title VII, the ADA, and the ADEA can help avoid liability when recruiting, hiring and promoting employees.

Conflict Resolution

Often, resolving workplace conflicts can be an emotional and complex experience with the potential for legal liability. Many diversity related disputes result in complaints of discrimination based on Title VII, the ADA and the ADEA if there is the perception that unfair treatment has occurred during the employment relationship or resolution process. Understanding the relevant laws can limit complaints and avoid liability when complaints are filed.

Different Generations

Today's workforce consists of employees from different generations, such as Baby Boomers, and Generations X and Y. Generational diversity is on the rise, along with complaints of age discrimination and unfair treatment based on age. To avoid age related complaints and liability, employers and supervisors need to understand the ADEA.

The legal ramifications underlying diversity management are important considerations in today's litigious society. It's essential for organizations to be proactive and provide periodic training on the diversity related laws. Such training can help to make these laws "legal friendly" and ensure that employers, supervisors and employees understand their legal responsibilities.

A CAREER AS AN AFFIRMATIVE ACTION OFFICER

Due to the increase in workforce diversity, concerns over complaints of employment harassment and discrimination, the litigious nature of our society, and the need to promote cooperation within the workplace, many organizations have recognized the need for having an in-house person available to resolve diversity related complaints and grievances filed by employees and job applicants. That person is sometimes referred to as an Affirmative Action Officer, Equal Employment Opportunity Officer, Diversity Director or some combination of those terms. The benefits resulting from the expertise of this person can far outweigh any cost incurred with the position. The affirmative action/equal employment opportunity function may be part of an organization's Human Resources department or in larger organizations, an entirely separate department. Some organizations have even outsourced this function. Nevertheless, the various roles of an Affirmative Action Officer require that s/he work collaboratively and interact with all departments within the organization and the community on diversity related matters.

Although an Affirmative Action Officer interacts with the community and employees at all levels of the organization, it is an unfamiliar and misunderstood career choice for many Human Resources students. Part of the reason has to do with the specialized and confidential nature of work being performed. Often the role of an Affirmative Action Officer in resolving a complaint is never known, except by those directly involved in the complaint. The public and most of the employees in the organization may not even be aware that a complaint existed in the first place or if they were aware, did not know the details. As a result, an organization may be effective in resolving discrimination complaints and avoiding litigation, but confidentiality concerns may limit public awareness.

Complaints by employees have become a frequent occurrence in many workplaces. No matter how much employees like their co-workers, jobs or supervisors, eventually disagreements are going to occur and conflict resolution will be necessary to promote cooperation and teamwork. However, when dealing with diversity, greater care must be exercised due to the potential for legal liability to result. Because there is no such thing as a typical case of discrimination, since every complaint is different and fact specific, the resolution process often requires creative problem-solving. However, resolving complaints can be a time-consuming process, especially when responding to the governmental agencies responsible for enforcing equal employment opportunity laws and administering affirmative action regulations. When governmental agencies become involved in a complaint, the resolution process generally results in greater scrutiny and paperwork. Also, complaints can be sporadic, such that an organization may not experience a complaint for months and then suddenly, experience several in a single week or short time frame.

An Affirmative Action Officer uses a variety of skills and abilities while performing the dual role of equal employment opportunity and affirmative action. Equal employment opportunity is a legal duty placed on the organization and includes the duty to investigate and resolve complaints of harassment and discrimination, and to ensure that employment decisions are based on objective and job related criteria. In this role, the Affirmative Action Officer can often prevent small problems from escalating into major ones, avoid costly litigation and negative publicity, and improve employee morale and retention. Because equal employment opportunity is required for most employers, it's essential that employers and supervisors understand what their responsibilities are.

On the other hand, affirmative action is a promise or commitment made by an employer to increase workplace diversity by being proactive in the recruitment, hiring and promotion of women, minorities, people with disabilities, and Vietnam Era veterans. Also, affirmative action is required for most government contractors. An employer must be an equal employment opportunity employer but not necessarily an affirmative action employer because equal employment opportunity is the law while affirmative action is not. Other functions of an Affirmative Action Officer include:

- Administering, enforcing and updating the organization's equal employment opportunity and affirmative action programs, policies and procedures to ensure compliance with federal, state and local laws.
- Developing and conducting training programs for the organization and community on the diversity related laws and issues.
- Serving as a resource person and advisor for the organization and community in areas related to equal employment opportunity, affirmative action and other diversity related matters.

The resolution of complaints can be a stressful and unappreciated aspect of the job, especially given the confidential nature of equal employment opportunity. However, it is also a very rewarding role given the value to the organization associated with the resolution process. Traditionally, the person performing the equal employment opportunity/affirmative action functions didn't require any specialized skills or training, however, that is no longer true today. Anyone interested in a career as an Affirmative Action Officer should pursue a curriculum in Human Resources, with emphasis on courses in employment laws and regulations, conflict resolution and diversity management. Also, having work related experience in an area of human resources is helpful, along with the ability to work with people.

IS THERE A NEED FOR AFFIRMATIVE ACTION?

It seems as though every year, there is discussion about whether affirmative action should be continued, modified, or eliminated all together. Because of the perceived impact affirmative action can have on hiring and promotion, it is one of the most controversial, emotional and misunderstood issues in diversity management. Consequently, there are vocal and staunch proponents and opponents of this 1965 governmental policy. Initially, affirmative action was supposed to be a short term policy designed to encourage organizations to take proactive steps to recruit, hire and promote qualified women and minorities and thereby diversify the workforce. However, opponents feel that the purpose of affirmative action has been fulfilled and that it has been in existence too long with no apparent end in sight. To understand affirmative action, it's important to examine both sides of the issue.

Argument against Affirmative Action

Reverse Discrimination

Affirmative action results in preferential treatment for women and minorities and thus, discriminates against white males and those groups not included in affirmative action. Considering someone's gender, race or ethnicity is discriminatory, unfair and contradictions equal employment opportunity, resulting in women and minorities benefiting at the expense of other groups, especially white males. Rather than encouraging lawful and ethical behavior toward women and minorities, affirmative action has had a divisive effect and increased tension between employees. Special treatment for some groups ultimately results in reverse discrimination for other groups.

Enough Progress

There has been enough progress made by women and minorities in terms of being hired and promoted. Women represent over 47 percent of the American labor force, and minorities and immigrants represent over 26 percent. Also, with the increasing amount of diversity in the American workforce, many believe that white males are quickly becoming a minority group, making affirmative action unnecessary and a waste of resources.

Focus on Equal Employment Opportunity

The focus of America's employment policy should be equal employment opportunity, not affirmative action. Equal employment opportunity emphasizes the use of objective and job related criteria when making employment decisions. Basing employment decisions on gender, race or ethnicity are not job related factors and therefore, violate the letter and spirit of equal opportunity. The effective enforcement of the equal employment opportunity laws is enough to achieve the purpose of affirmative action.

More Government Regulation

Affirmative action is just another example of unnecessary government regulation. It is time consuming, costly to administer, confusing, divisive, creates endless paperwork, and offers no real benefits for organizations. Considering the degree of global competition that exist today, government efforts should be directed toward helping organizations compete, rather than presenting obstacles.

Long Term Policy

Although, affirmative action was initially developed as a short term diversity oriented policy, it has been in existence for over 40 years. Forty years is not short term for any generation of employees who do not receive preferential treatment under affirmative action. Today's younger generation of employees should not be penalized for employment discrimination that occurred generations ago. Also, harassment and discrimination are not only experienced by women and minorities, everyone has been a victim of unfair treatment at some point in their lives.

Arguments for Affirmative Action

Still Needed

Affirmative action is needed because there has not been enough progress made by women and minorities in hiring and promotion. Unfortunately, prejudicial behavior, harassment and discrimination are still common occurrences in many organizations. Consequently, the equal employment opportunity laws need to be supplemented with affirmative action in order to ensure equal opportunity for women and minorities in the workplace.

Proactive Policy

Affirmative action can help organizations avoid problems by encouraging them to thoroughly consider their employment decisions and actions. It can limit harassment and discrimination complaints and lawsuits from occurring by providing the incentive for organizations to be proactive in recruiting, hiring and promoting qualified women and minorities.

Voluntary Policy

Most affirmative action is not required by the law, but voluntarily undertaken by employers. For example, Title VII of the 1964 Civil Right Act does not require or prohibit affirmative action. Also, most employers do not have affirmative action programs. Therefore, the majority of organizations that have affirmative action programs have done so voluntarily due to the benefits associated with it.

Limited Application

Many opponents of affirmative action are not aware that it has limited application in employment decision making. For the most part, affirmative action only applies to the recruiting, hiring and promotion decisions of those companies that are government contractors. All other aspects of employment decision making are not affected by affirmative action.

Short Term Policy

Affirmative action is not going to continue forever. It was originally designed as a short term remedy or incentive to ensure that women and minorities are not overlooked in the hiring and promotion process. Although the policy has been in existence for over 40 years, discrimination and harassment have existed for centuries. Forty years of affirmative action is short term compared to over 200 years of discrimination.

Benefits Exceed Costs

There are more benefits resulting from affirmative action than costs associated with it. Some of the benefits include: more diversity in the workforce, advancement opportunities for women, minorities, and persons with disabilities, correcting for the effects of past discrimination, fewer discrimination complaints and lawsuits, and qualifying for lucrative government contracts. The benefits of ensuring that traditionally underutilized groups will be part of an organization's workforce exceed the costs involved. Also, even for those people who are not members of a protected group, they can realize the benefits of affirmative action through employment opportunities for their spouses, daughters and relatives who have disabilities, are veterans or married to minorities.

Regardless of whether you support or oppose affirmative action, it will continue to be a source of controversy for organizations. Therefore, management needs to be aware of the arguments for and against affirmative action, and prepared to effectively deal with the issue.

REVIEW QUESTIONS

1. Affirmative action is a legal duty for most employers.
2. The ADEA of 1967 prohibits all age discrimination in employment.
3. Executive Order 11246 requires affirmative action for women.
4. An employee who believes he/she is experiencing (workplace) race discrimination can file a discrimination complaint under Title VII.
5. Affirmative action quotas are legal if an employer has an affirmative action plan.
6. If an affirmative action goal exists for a given position, the employer is still allowed to hire the best qualified person for the position even if that person is not a goal satisfying person.
7. Equal employment opportunity is considered to be a long term policy for the U.S.
8. An employer needs affirmative action (plan) to qualify for a contract to provide goods or services to the federal government.
9. What is an example of "reverse discrimination?"
10. Why is an affirmative action plan a defensive tool when responding to complaints of employment discrimination?

LEARNING ACTIVITIES

1. Divide the class into teams and assign each team an affirmative action issue or concern to discuss.
2. Assign different students or teams of students to provide arguments supporting and opposing affirmative action, and how affirmative action might be improved.

Issue Three

Stereotyping, Prejudice, and Discrimination

"Don't focus on only one aspect but see the total person"

Issue Three deals with a common occurrence when meeting someone new or interacting with co-workers who are perceived to be "different," discrimination. Closely related to the issue of discrimination are stereotyping and prejudice. Unfortunately, these concerns continue to be workplace problems that can negatively impact relationships, supervision and organizational performance.

Being aware of the fact that stereotyping, prejudice and discrimination occur, and the reasons why are major steps in dealing with those issues. Also, when thinking about people, we need to focus on the total person and not on only one aspect of that person. Fortunately, we have the ability to manage or change our thinking about how we perceive people who are different from us. Because prejudice toward certain individuals and groups involves attitudes that are learned, we can unlearn those negative attitudes and learn new ones.

UNFORTUNATELY, INDIVIDUALS IN ALL GROUPS ARE STEREOTYPED

People are taught or conditioned to think and behave in certain ways. We have been conditioned to believe that if two things look the same on the outside, they must be the same on the inside. For example, one bottle of Coca Cola soda pop is the same as another, both on the outside and inside. One McDonald's Big Mac hamburger is the same as another, outside and inside. Since childhood, most of us have been conditioned to generalize and believe that if two things look similar, then they must be the same. Unfortunately, some of us apply this reasoning when interacting with other people. When applied to people this conditioning often leads to faulty assumptions, negative stereotyping and discrimination.

Some people believe that all members of a given ethnic group are the same. For example, because they have common outward characteristics or similarities in appearance, it is assumed that all members of an ethnic group must be the same on the inside, with each individual of that group possessing the same feelings, needs, and personalities. Consequently, we tend to stereotype members of cultural and ethnic groups, along with people from the same generation and gender. In today's workplace, the diversity of the workforce presents supervisors with the challenge of how to resist stereotyping employees in order to effectively manage them.

An additional concern for supervisors and employees is overcoming the belief that only individuals in certain ethnic or racial groups are stereotyped and discriminated against, while individuals of other groups are not. Unfortunately, all of us have been victims of prejudice and discrimination in one form or another. No individual or group has a monopoly on experiencing unfair treatment and discrimination based on negative stereotyping, prejudice, and misinformation.

Consequently, negative stereotyping and discrimination are not only experienced by people in minority groups, but by individuals of all groups. For example, young, white males experience negative stereotyping and discrimination, just as individuals of minority groups do. At the same time, there are some who believe that negative stereotyping and unfair treatment is politically acceptable when it is applied to "young, white males, without visible disabilities."

In fact, early diversity awareness training programs would often negatively stereotype white males and accuse them of being responsible for most workplace difficulties. Typically, white males were criticized and blamed for diversity related problems and held accountable for improving workplace relationships, while individuals of many other groups were not held to the same standards of accountability. Consequently, many believed white males had the primary responsibility to change and adjust their attitudes in order to promote workforce diversity.

Assuming that all white males think and behave alike is not only inaccurate, but also unfair and ethically wrong. Stereotyping white males is just as unfair as stereotyping women, minorities, or people with disabilities. Just as personalities differ among women, minorities and people with disabilities, there is diversity among white males. We must remember that white males represent a significant part of organizational and societal diversity. The benefits of America's diverse workforce would be less if there were no white males in it. Therefore, promoting diversity is the responsibility everyone and we all need to examine our attitudes to ensure nondiscriminatory behavior and equal opportunity for everybody.

Although there are laws against certain types of discrimination in the workplace, employment discrimination still occurs. At the same time, employees who belong to protected groups account for over 70 percent of the U.S. workforce and represent the majority of employees who file discrimination complaints. The irony is that in one sense, the majority in the workforce, the 70 percent, are protected by laws from the minority, the 30 percent who are not in protected groups.

It's important to note that the differences between individuals in various ethnic groups, and even races, have become blurred in recent years because of increases in interracial and interethnic families and children. Families and individuals in our country are a mixture of many races, cultures and ethnicities. Also, our uniqueness and individuality is made up of the different aspects of many groups that we belong to or choose to identify with. At the same time, regardless of someone's genealogy, background, or appearance, each individual will place different values on characteristics associated with certain groups. Consequently, it's becoming more common for individuals to check the "multiracial" category or identification on job applications and government information forms.

Globalization is placing greater emphasis on organizational cooperation. Everyone must assume the responsibility for working together. Therefore, for organizational survival, eliminating stereotyping and discrimination is the responsibility of every employee. Managing diversity requires that each person assume the responsibility for eliminating negative stereotyping, prejudice and discrimination. As supervisors, we need to recognize and appreciate each employee as an individual, regardless of his/her ethnic or social classification. As supervisors, we need to act as role models and influence the attitudes and behaviors of employees in positive ways. By placing emphasis on the individual and avoiding negative stereotyping, American organizations can prosper in the global economy and at the same time ensure equal opportunity for all employees.

DEALING WITH STEREOTYPING AND PREJUDICE
IN THE WORKPLACE

As is true with books, many of us tend to make judgments about others based on appearance or what we see. Even though we know that physical appearance is not a reliable criterion for evaluating people, it's difficult for many of us to resist our cultural conditioning. As a result, an employee's appearance can lead to stereotyping, prejudice and discrimination.

Stereotyping occurs when we assign specific traits to an individual based on physical appearance or perceived membership in a specific group. We have been conditioned to believe that if two things look the same on the outside, they must have the same contents on the inside. Although this may be true with various standardized brand name products, it is not true for people. For example, although people who belong to a given ethnic group may have a similar physical appearance, each individual of that group does not think or act alike. Each individual is unique and different from everyone else in that group.

Closely related to stereotyping is prejudice. Prejudice is a negative attitude we have about a certain group or members of that group. Overcoming prejudice is important for relationship development because this attitude can often lead to misunderstanding and discrimination. Identifying the major reasons or sources for prejudice can help us to understand and overcome it.

Sources of Prejudice

Fear of Differences

What we don't understand or are unfamiliar with, we tend to fear and avoid. Most people have a preference for a certain degree of certainty and predictability in their lives. The lack of information about someone can create misunderstanding and fear which in turn can cause people to feel uncomfortable and react emotionally, rather than objectively. For example, if an employee's physical appearance is distinctly different from ours, we become fearful and prefer not to associate or work with that employee.

Competition

Although competition can be a source of motivation, it can also have certain negative consequences if not properly managed. For example, research shows that whenever individuals or groups are regularly placed in direct competition with each other for something of value, such as jobs, promotions or salary, this may eventually result in dislike for one another over time. When it comes to jobs or salaries, poor economic conditions have a tendency to increase the degree of prejudice and discrimination experienced in the workplace than when conditions are prosperous.

Social Learning

Unfortunately, most prejudice is learned. As children, we learned the attitudes and values of our parents, relatives and close friends, and likewise learned how to think about and treat people who were different. This conditioning often affects us as adults. Consequently, employees who are prejudice toward other groups were not born that way, but learned those attitudes.

Ethnocentrism

Ethnocentrism is an extreme belief that our culture, group or nation is better or more correct than other cultures, groups or nations. It's an extreme belief because we tend to believe that only our culture has the right values or represents the right way to behave.

Reducing Stereotyping and Prejudice

Because stereotyping and prejudice are learned, we can develop strategies to reduce it in the workplace. The following actions can be used to reduce stereotyping and prejudice in the workplace:

- Provide diversity training to help make supervisors and employees aware of the benefits of workforce diversity and understand how to deal with people with different cultural values. Supervisors and employees need to change how they view co-workers who are different and recognize the benefits that diverse thinking can provide.
- Supervisor need to exercise flexible leadership when dealing with diverse employees. The guide for effective interpersonal relationships is to treat employees as individuals by taking the time and making the effort to learn about how each employee wants to be treated. Employees should be treated as equals, but not necessarily the same.
- Provide training on the relevant diversity related employment laws. In today's litigious society and diverse workforce, supervisors must be aware of their legal responsibilities and the consequences of their decision making. Training on the anti-discrimination laws can force supervisors and employees to think about how their attitudes and behavior affect others and thereby, limit complaints and costly litigation.
- Encourage diversity role models. Supervisors can influence the attitudes and behavior of employees. Therefore, to promote an inclusive work environment, supervisors should act as role models by demonstrating positive attitudes and behaviors toward all employees.
- Evaluate employees on objective and job related criteria. The use of objective and job related criteria will help ensure fairness and accurate performance

evaluations. Such standards will also encourage high performance and limit complaints of discrimination.

- Provide mentors to advise employees on making the best career decisions and increase their opportunities for success. It must be recognized that employee success is not only based on technical competency, but also on interpersonal skills and networking. Also, mentoring can be an important component of recruiting and retention initiatives.

FUNCTIONS OF STEREOTYPING

When people interact with one another, they tend to stereotype or categorize each other by assigning specific traits based on physical appearance or perceived membership in specific groups. Stereotyping, such as making judgments about people based on certain physical characteristics, affects relationship development in several ways. During the course of a relationship, stereotyping may occur at different times and serve different functions. Regardless of how we feel about stereotyping, it occurs, impacts organizational teamwork and performance, and therefore, we must learn how to deal with it. To overcome negative stereotyping, we need to understand its functions.

Principal Functions of Stereotyping

First Impressions

People often use stereotyping to form a first impression about someone they just met. During an initial encounter, we know very little about each other and form first impressions based on assumptions and stereotypes. Stereotyping people based on their appearance or perceived membership in certain groups may set the stage for initial conversation and the beginning of a relationship. However, we must exercise care because first impressions often have lasting effects and stereotyping may have a negative impact on relationship development. Awareness of how unfair and inaccurate stereotypes are can help us to keep an open mind about people and prevent first impressions from becoming negative and permanent beliefs.

Individual Identity

Some people rely on stereotyping for recognition or identification purposes. Stereotyping is sometimes used to identify or define "who a person is" based on the different groups that person is perceived to belong to. Perceptions about a person, based on group affiliation, may or may not reflect reality, but nonetheless, affects relationship development. Although each individual will determine how closely he/she chooses to identify with a given group, once the stereotype is established, it will generally be difficult to overcome. Fortunately, the cultural and ethnic categories we traditionally placed people into are becoming more blurred due to the fact that people are rejecting the stereotypes that are sometimes associated with them, the amount of intermarriage taking place, and the number of multiracial or multicultural people that exist.

Simplify Human Behavior

Understanding people can be difficult, especially when interacting with people from different cultural backgrounds. A person's thinking, behavior, and personality tend to be influenced by the different groups he/she belongs to. Recognizing this, we sometimes rely on stereotypes to replace information gaps about people and facilitate our understanding of them. By simplifying and generalizing about why people think and behave the way they do, we tend to believe we can better understand them, ourselves and human behavior. However, we need to be aware that the obvious stereotypes we have about people can be misleading and result in misunderstanding about individual behavior and people in general.

Awareness of Differences

Given the degree of diversity that exists in society and the workplace, the average person will have numerous opportunities to interact with people from various cultures and backgrounds. Stereotyping can creates awareness of these differences and force us to think about them. Sometimes, this awareness of differences results in prejudice and discrimination, thus, having a negative affect on relationship development. However, rather than viewing differences in a negative light, we can choose to view diversity as a benefit. If we take the time and make the effort to understand the advantages that differences can provide, ethnocentrism and discrimination can be reduced.

Justify Behavior

Some people rely on stereotyping to justify their behavior toward others. We treat people the way we do based on our beliefs or stereotypes about them. For example, some employers pay women and minorities less than employees of other groups for doing the same job based on the false belief that women and minorities are not as qualified, competent or productive. Older job applicants may not be hired for certain jobs, especially technical positions, because of the stereotype that they do not have the desire or ability to learn new skills. Sometimes people with disabilities are not hired because of the belief that they can't do a particular job. Discrimination based on stereotypes can be avoided if we choose to think and behave differently toward people. Awareness that discrimination is learned behavior can help us to better understand ourselves and choose to behave in a nondiscriminatory manner. Any behavior that is learned can be unlearned, and replaced by a new and more positive behavior.

Although stereotyping is a common occurrence, it is subjective, misleading and does not consider individual differences among people. As a result, assigning people to certain groups based on their appearance or perceived group membership often has negative effects on relationship development and can make it difficult for employees to effectively work together. For positive relationship development, each person should be viewed and treated as an individual. Thinking positive about people who are different and having an open mind about them, along with the willingness to learn from those we perceive as different, can facilitate the development of an inclusive attitude.

OVERCOMING MISPERCEPTIONS ABOUT EMPLOYMENT DISCRIMINATION

Any discussion about diversity or managing diversity would not be complete without an understanding of employment discrimination and the laws regulating this area. Questionable decisions or the perception of unfair treatment are the cornerstones for most discrimination complaints and lawsuits filed by employees against their employers, supervisors and co-workers.

Newspaper headlines about million dollar verdicts rendered against employers due to workplace discrimination highlight the potential liability associated with such illegal behavior. Understanding the anti-discrimination laws is the key to preventing discrimination and avoiding liability. Unfortunately, these laws have been a constant source of confusion and misunderstanding for many employers and supervisors since their inception. One way to understand the anti-discrimination laws is to explore some of the common myths and false perceptions about employment discrimination.

Ten Misperceptions About Employment Discrimination

1. The anti-discrimination laws prohibit all employment discrimination.

One of the major misperceptions concerning employment discrimination is that the antidiscrimination laws prohibit all employment discrimination. In reality, these laws only prohibit certain types of employment discrimination, specifically, discrimination based on race, color, religion, national origin, gender, disability and age. An additional complication is that there is often a fine line between behaviors that are legal and illegal. Employment discrimination has many gray areas which often leave employers questioning their actions and decisions.

A related concern is to distinguish between employment actions or decisions that is unfair and illegal with those that are unfair and legal. What is unfair is not necessarily illegal. There are some behaviors, actions or decisions that are legal, some that are outright illegal and others that are perceived as unfair, but legal. Table 3.1 illustrates these three situations.

Table 3.1.   Legal versus Illegal Decisions

Legal decisions (using objective & job related criteria	Legal decisions (using subjective & non-job related criteria)	Illegal decisions (using subjective & non-job related criteria)
Decisions based on skills, experience, education, etc. disability, age	Decisions based on height, weight, sexual orientation, etc.	Decisions based on race, color, religion, national origin, gender,

For example, basing an employment decision on a person's sexual orientation, height, weight or other subjective non-job related criterion may be unfair, but not illegal under federal law. Also, an employee's perception often comes into play when defining unfair treatment. "Fairness" is subjective, meaning that what is fair or not fair depends on one's perspective.

2. To avoid liability, employers and supervisors need to treat employees of protected groups better than employees who are not in such groups.

This is a common belief held by many employers and supervisors that is primarily based on the confusion and fear about the antidiscrimination laws. These laws do not require preferential treatment for employees in protected groups. Instead, the antidiscrimination laws prohibit unfair treatment based on someone's race, color, religion and other protected characteristics. In other words, employers and supervisors are supposed to treat or consider protected characteristics as neutral factors when making employment decisions.

Historically speaking, it was common for race, gender and other protected characteristics to negatively influence employment decision making.

Giving women and members of minority groups preferential treatment can result in complaints and lawsuits of reverse discrimination by white males who may be adversely affected by such favorable treatment. Also, from an ethical standpoint, we should not base our behavior or employment decisions on group affiliation, but on individuality.

3. Employers are only liable for discrimination committed by supervisors and employees.

Employers can be held liable for employment discrimination committed by supervisors, employees and non-employees who enter the workplace. Consequently, employers must maintain a work environment free from harassment and discrimination by anyone who enters the workplace. For example, employers have a legal duty to protect employees from harassment and discrimination by customers, vendors, suppliers, repairpersons and anyone else that enters the workplace.

4. The anti-discrimination laws place severe restrictions on an employer's right to establish workplace rules.

Because the majority of employer-employee relationships are based on the "at will" employment doctrine, employers generally have the right to establish whatever workplace rules the employer desires with few restrictions. As long as workplace rules are consistently enforced and do not discriminate based on race, color, religion and other protected characteristics, an employer is free to establish any objective or even subjective workplace rule.

5. The type of employment discrimination most employees experience today is similar to what was encountered in the past.

One effect of changing laws and society's views of unfair treatment is that discrimination has become less obvious. Most of the employment discrimination occurring today is more subtle than what it was in the past. For example, in the past it was common for an employer to refuse to hire a woman because she was pregnant or might become pregnant, prohibit women from working in production jobs because they were women, or to require employees to retire once they reached a certain age. Although sex and age discrimination still occur, it's not as obvious or prevalent as it once was.

Instead, most workplace discrimination involves subtle and less obvious behavior. For example, not hiring someone with the pretext that the person is "overqualified" for the position he/she is applying for may be considered as age discrimination when applied to someone 40 or over in age. Theoretically, employers should want to hire the best qualified person, meaning they should want to hire someone who exceeds the minimum qualifications required for the job. The higher the qualifications an applicant has, the more qualified that applicant should be for the job. Therefore the applicant with the highest qualifications should be offered the position. Another example is not allowing women to work at certain jobs or in certain workplace areas because there are known hazards present that may harm them. However, this is a pretext for gender discrimination because if a job or area is hazardous for women, then it would be hazardous for men as well.

6. Employees who file complaints or lawsuits against their employers have a high probability of winning those complaints or lawsuits.

Alleging discrimination and proving it are two different things. In order to prevail in a lawsuit, the plaintiff or person alleging a violation of his/her rights must provide evidence which will prove by a preponderance of evidence that discrimination took place. It can be difficult for an employee to prove discrimination since:

- witnesses (if there are any) are often co-workers or supervisors who are likely to side with the employer
- documentation, such as personnel files and performance appraisals, is held by the employer, and
- employers have the financial resources to hire the best legal services
- Consequently, the majority of discrimination complaints and lawsuits filed against employers are decided in favor of employers.

7. The anti-discrimination laws only protect women, minorities and others members of protected groups.

Who are the victims of discrimination? The answer is that everyone has the potential to become a victim. Although some groups experience discrimination more often than others, no one or group is free from stereotyping, prejudice or discrimination. Consequently, the laws are designed to protect everyone from discrimination, including white males. Federal laws prohibit employers from basing employment decisions on race, color, religion, national origin, gender, disability and age. Also, complaints and lawsuits of reverse discrimination can be filed, where white males allege that they have been discriminated because of their race or gender. Just as diversity includes white males, the anti-discrimination laws also protect white males.

8. Affirmative action is a type of reverse discrimination against white males.

In some regards affirmative action is the exception to the general rule that race or gender should not be taken into consideration when making employment decisions. Equal employment opportunity is the general rule of law and requires that race or gender be neutral factors during decision making. Under limited circumstances, affirmative action does allow employers to use race or gender as a "plus factor" when making hiring and promotion decisions. At the same time, affirmative action is not a legal duty and therefore, an employer has the right to hire the best qualified person for a position, whether that person is a member of a protected group or not.

9. Laws are the best ways to prevent employment discrimination.

History demonstrates that laws alone cannot effectively mandate morality, ethical behavior or attitudes. Laws serve to establish minimum standards of acceptable behavior and provide remedies for provable cases of discrimination. To prevent prejudice and discrimination, businesses must go beyond what the law prohibits and attack prejudice and discrimination at its origin. Education and training can help to make people aware of why they are prejudice and therefore, engage in discriminatory behavior. Because prejudice and discrimination are learned, it can be unlearned through diversity education.

10. Employers and supervisors must become lawyers or have extensive legal training to understand and avoid violating the various federal, state and municipal anti-discrimination laws.

Certainly, one way for employers and supervisors to understand the law and their legal responsibilities is to know all of the various antidiscrimination laws that exist. However, even with legal knowledge, laws change and continuous updating will be necessary. The easiest way to avoid violating the antidiscrimination laws is for employers and supervisors to base every employment decision on objective and job related criteria.

REVIEW QUESTIONS

1. When people first meet, they tend to first notice the other person's age.
2. Most people tend to remember what they hear longer than what they see.
3. Americans generally do not make judgment about others based on appearance.
4. People who are prejudice were most likely born that way.
5. Encouraging ethnocentrism is an effective way to reduce prejudice.
6. Prejudice is an attitude based on misinformation.
7. A major source of prejudice is competition.
8. Today, stereotyping non-minority males is acceptable in most diversity training programs.
9. Most stereotypes about certain social, ethical and cultural groups are true.
10. Most prejudice has a common denominator.

LEARNING ACTIVITIES

1. Divide the class into teams and assign each team a set of minority/cultural stereotypes to be discussed.
2. Require each student to identify a situation where he/she was a victim of stereotyping and the consequences of that situation.

Issue Four

Women in the Workplace

"Women have become one of the most significant components of work-force diversity"

Issue Four deals with what many experts believe to be the most significant component of managing diversity, women. Awareness of the number of women in the workforce, the progress women have made in the workplace and how they have influenced employment related laws, and company policies and practices, highlights the importance of this issue. Any discussion or study of the management of diversity would not be complete without an understanding of the role women have in the workplace.

Most of the factors that encouraged women to enter the workforce in the past are still present today. Consequently, as more women enter the workforce and assume management positions, gender related issues will continue to dominate the attention of employers and supervisors. Gender related issues are not only important for U.S. employers, but for employers throughout the world. Unfortunately, despite the progress women have made, gender harassment and discrimination remain as common workplace concerns.

HISTORY CAN PROMOTE UNDERSTANDING

In the minds of many diversity experts, women represent the most significant component of organizational diversity. The employment of women has had a major impact on organizational policies, workplace culture, and employment laws that continue to affected all employees and organizations. Knowing the historical employment patterns of American women can help to identify their current concerns and roles in the workplace. Also, awareness of how the roles of women have evolved over time can promote understanding and improve relationships between male and female supervisors and employees.

Pre-industrial Period

During the Pre-industrial Era (1776-1789), the American home was considered to be the center of production and analogous with today's workplace. Everything the family needed, from a material standpoint, was handmade and produced at home. Men and women played an equal role in producing food, clothing, household items and other necessities of life. Women shared an equal role with men in contributing to the material and economic well being of the average household. The Pre-industrial period can be considered to be a "period of economic parity for American women" because the economic contributions of women were at least equal to that of men.

Industrial Period

The Industrial Revolution (1800) had a profound effect on the U.S. and changed the role of women in society and the workplace. During this time period, the center of production moved from the home and into the newly built factories. People began working outside the home on a regular basis and money became a necessity of life. Whatever material needs the family required could be satisfied with money. Various sociological and biological arguments were used to encourage men to work in the factories and at the same time, discourage women from working outside the home.

For example, it was thought that women should not work outside the home because the workplace was dangerous, required physical strength, was psychologically stressful, and women didn't have or couldn't learn the appropriate skills. As a result, few women, in comparison to men, worked outside the home. The small percentage of women who did work outside the home on a full-time basis were considered to be temporary workers, composed primarily of young and singled women. As this pattern of women employment continued, the economic contribution of what women did, both at home and in the workplace, declined.

World Wars

During World War I (1917–1918), there was a critical shortage of workers for the American factories. As a result, women were encouraged to enter the workforce and contribute to the war effort. Unfortunately for the progress of women in the workforce, once the war ended and the men returned, the majority of women who had entered the workplace during the war went back to being homemakers.

During World War II (1941–1945), as was true during World War I, there was a critical shortage of workers for the factories. Once again, women entered the factories to fill the needs of production and support the war effort. However, after World War II ended, a large percentage of women who entered the workforce during the war remained. Consequently, women participation in the American workforce has continued to increase ever since.

Today

Today, women represent over 47 percent of the American labor force, with married women representing the largest percent of the female workforce. Over the last 40 years, several factors have contributed to the increase in women participation in the workforce, including:

Economic Factors

To maintain and improve the family standard of living, more women have entered the workforce. The two-income family, where both spouses work, has become common. Also, the increase in divorced and singled women has encouraged women to pursue employment opportunities.

Educational Factors

Education qualifies people for more jobs by improving their skill level and making them more marketable. Women have recognized the importance of education as a means for attaining a career and independence. As the educational levels for women have increased, so have their participation in the workforce.

Life Style Factors

The number of years women devote to childbearing and childrearing have declined due to various sociological and personal reasons while their average life spans have risen. As a result, women have more time available to do other things, such as working and pursuing careers opportunities.

Attitudes

Societal attitudes influence the workplace. Because social attitudes about women have changed, America's attitudes about women working outside the home have also changed. Consequently, the changed attitudes by spouses, employers, and co-workers concerning women and work have contributed to more women entering the workforce.

Laws

Since 1963, several laws, considered to be "women-friendly," have contributed to more women entering the workforce.

- The Equal Pay Act of 1963, requires that men and women performing the same job are to receive the same compensation.
- Title VII of the 1964 Civil Rights Act, prohibits discrimination in employment based on race, color, religion, national origin, and gender.
- The Pregnancy Discrimination Act of 1978, prohibits discrimination in employment based on pregnancy, childbirth and related conditions.
- The Family and Medical Leave Act of 1993, allows employees up to 12 weeks of unpaid leave for family related or medical emergencies.
- Executive Order 11246, requires employers with federal contracts to use proactive strategies to recruit, hire, and promote women and minorities.

Although the above mentioned laws are often thought of as only benefiting women, when in reality, all employees and families benefit from these laws. For example, these laws provide benefits for married men, men with daughters, and men with girlfriends and sisters.

The contributions of women in the workforce are being recognized and valued. Unfortunately, women still experience prejudicial behavior, harassment and discrimination at all levels in many organizations. For example, the average female employee earns only $.76 for every dollar the average male earns. Nevertheless, women will continue to be an important part of organizational diversity and success. Managing diversity will ensure that all employees, including women employees, have an opportunity to realize their potential and help the organization prosper in the global economy.

SEXUAL HARASSMENT COMES IN TWO VARIETIES

Despite the progress women have made in the workplace and the existence of employment policies and laws, sexual harassment continues to be a common and serious problem for many organizations. Unfortunately, there is much misunderstanding on what behaviors constitute sexual harassment and what employers can do to limit complaints and lawsuits resulting from it.

Sexual harassment is a form of employment discrimination, under both federal and state antidiscrimination laws, because the harasser treats his/her victim(s) unfairly based on their gender. The law imposes a duty on employers to maintain a workplace free of employment discrimination, including sexual harassment. Employers may be held responsible for sexual harassment committed by supervisors, co-workers and even non-employees (such as customers, vendors and suppliers who come into contact with employees during working hours) if appropriate preventive and corrective actions are not taken.

The legal remedies available to victims of sexual harassment include monetary awards under state personal injury laws for assault and battery, invasion of privacy, and infliction of emotional distress. There are additional remedies available under federal law, specifically, Title VII of the 1964 Civil Rights Act. Although women are the overwhelming victims of sexual harassment, men have also been subjected to such illegal behaviors on occasions. Consequently, both men and women are protected by the law and have the right to file complaints with their employers, state and government enforcement agencies, and the courts.

"Sexual harassment is any unwelcome verbal or physical conduct of a sexual nature that adversely interferes with an employee's job." More specifically, the law recognizes two types of sexual harassment: Quid Pro Quo Sexual Harassment and Hostile Work Environment Sexual Harassment.

Quid Pro Quo (meaning "this for that") harassment is a type of sexual extortion and occurs when an employee is forced to grant sexual favors in return for job opportunities, such as promotion, pay raises or continued employment. A typical example is when an employee is threatened with termination if he/she refuses the sexual advances or demands of a supervisor. Quid Pro Quo Sexual Harassment can only be committed by someone in a power or decision-making position, such as an employer or supervisor. Because the employee/victim suffers a tangible employment action, employers are usually strictly liable when this type of harassment occurs. In other words, there is no defense available for the employer to avoid liability once this type of harassment occurs.

Hostile Work Environment Sexual Harassment occurs when an employee feels hassled, degraded and humiliated due to a work environment plagued by offensive behaviors of a sexual nature. This type of harassment may involve a variety of unwelcome behaviors, including; sexual jokes, flirtation, touching, pressure for dates or sex, sexual comments about one's physical appearance, the constant use of terms of endearment and online harassment. Over the course of time, these offensive behaviors begin to adversely interfere with an employee's job performance until the employee either quits the job or is terminated.

Hostile Work Environment Sexual Harassment can be committed by almost anyone who enters the workplace, including supervisors, co-workers and non-employees. Generally, Hostile Work Environment harassment is more difficult to prove than Quid Pro Quo harassment because the former doesn't involve an exchange of sexual favors for employment benefits. Nor does the law generally consider an isolated instance of offensive behavior illegal. Because tangible employment actions are not a consequence of Hostile Work Environment harassment, there are defenses available to the employer that may avoid or limit liability if this type of harassment occurs.

Due to the large number of women entering the workforce in recent decades, the incidences of sexual harassment have increased. As problems associated with sexual harassment escalate and continue to receive more attention, employers are being forced to take measures to prevent and correct sexual harassment. What can employers do to prevent and correct sexual harassment in the workplace?

- First, employers need to raise the issue of sexual harassment by having a written company policy against it, along with specific remedies and penalties for violations. It's important that every supervisor and employee be aware of this policy and the resulting sanctions. Posting the policy throughout the workplace can help to raise awareness of it, not only among employees, but also non-employees who enter the workplace.
- Second, regular training programs should be conducted to inform supervisors and employees of the company policy and behaviors that constitute sexual harassment. There should be two types of training provided:
  (1) Awareness training: to describe the policy and types of sexual harassment, along with examples of behaviors that constitute sexual harassment. Raising awareness can avoid harassment incidences and liability.
  (2) Sensitivity training: to help employees realize that different people perceive sexual harassment in different ways. For example, men generally feel less threaten by sexual harassment than women.
  Also, sexual harassment should be a topic of discussion with new employees to ensure they are aware and understand the policy.
- Finally, an in-house grievance or complaint procedure should be made available to enable victims of sexual harassment to complain and seek assistance in dealing with alleged harassment situations. Several important components should be included in this complaint procedure:
  (1) where and how to file complaints
  (2) investigation of complaints

(3) document every aspect of the complaint process
(4) confidentiality of complaints and the investigation
(5) "due process" or fairness during the process for the alleged victim and harasser
(6) corrective action to remedy the situation and prevent further harassment

Combating sexual harassment is a major challenge confronting today's employers. The problems associated with sexual harassment require employers to be proactive and implement both preventive and corrective measures to avoid liability. This is especially significant given the fact that more women are entering the workplace, employees are more aware of their legal rights, contact with non-employees has become more frequent due to the service economy, and more men are experiencing harassment and filing complaints. Preventing and correcting sexual harassment in the workplace should not be viewed as merely a favor provided to employees. Instead, it is a legal duty placed on employers and enforced by the law.

ROMANTIC RELATIONSHIPS IN THE WORKPLACE

Because men and women are spending more time at work, the workplace has become a common place for romantic relationships between employees to develop. As more men and women date and marry people they meet at work, the workplace will continue to be the principal meeting and dating location of the new millennium. Additionally, the service economy has resulted in more interactions between employees and non-employees, such as customers, thus creating more potential dating partners. Also, due to the extent of computer technology and employees engaged in personal online activities while at work, there will be further opportunities for employees to interact with each other and with non-employees. Consequently, there are now more opportunities for employees to meet and date co-workers and non-employees. According to research, three out of every five employees have had at least one romantic relationship with a co-worker and over 40 percent of couples met while on the job.

There are additional reasons why the workplace has become a common place for romantic relationships to develop. Since the average adult will spend approximately one-third of his or her time at work, the workplace offers prospective dating partners advantages that other gathering places or ways of meeting people do not. In addition to the number and variety of potential dating partners encountered on the job, dating a co-worker offers other benefits:

- knowing that a dating partner has a job
- opportunity to observe and learn about a dating partner on a daily basis
- can collect and verify personal information about a dating partner from co-workers
- on-the-job interaction between couples can create an inexpensive form of "dating"
- the relationship can develop naturally over time

However, workplace romances can also create workplace or performance related problems and legal concerns for employers, including:

- an uncomfortable work relationship when the romantic relationship ends
- poor performance by the employees involved in the relationship
- claims of inappropriate behavior and favoritism
- negative company image and publicity
- complaints of sexual harassment

Recognizing the potential problems associated with employees dating each other, do employers have the legal right to prohibit or regulate such consensual relationships between employees? The answer is a resounding yes! Employers have a legitimate business interest in regulating relationships in the workplace, including consensual romantic relationships. Although regulating consensual relationships in the workplace may initially appear to be an extreme and intrusive management prerogative, in today's litigious society it is necessary from a liability standpoint. Also, because most employees are considered to be "at will," employers can generally impose whatever work related rules the employer's desires, with few exceptions.

Although the sexual harassment laws prohibit only "unwelcome" sexual attention in the workplace, employers should discourage all sexual attention during working hours. The idea that romantic relationships between employees may promote workplace harmony and teamwork are outweighed by the potential problems such relationships may create. Because relationships can have sudden and unhappy endings, behaviors that are welcomed and consensual one day may become unwelcome and illegal the next day. In other words, today's consensual romantic relationship may become tomorrow's sexual harassment complaint.

Due to the potential problems resulting from workplace romances, some employers have instituted both a sexual harassment policy, which prohibit illegal (unwelcome) sexual behavior in the workplace and a non-fraternization policy, for regulating (consensual) employee dating. Just as sexual harassment policies vary from one organization to another, so do non-fraternization policies.

For example, an employer's non-fraternization policy may prohibit co-workers from dating entirely or prohibit dating between certain categories of employees, such as between supervisors and subordinates. However, any policy on employees dating should be as least restrictive as possible, in order to avoid misunderstandings, enforcement problems and complaints of invasion of privacy. At a minimum, a non-fraternization policy should discourage romantic relationships between supervisors and subordinates in the same department and encourage all employees to behave in a professional manner while at work.

Related employment policies some employers are implementing to restrict employee dating are conflict of interest policies. As applied to dating, these policies are designed to prevent problems that may arise if employees date customers or clients.

As is true when establishing any company policy, employers need to provide training to inform supervisors and the employees about why such policies are necessary. While a sexual harassment and non-fraternization policy may limit employee dating, these policies will not eliminate workplace romances entirely. History cites numerous examples of the extremes people will go to initiate and continue romantic relationships. However, by being proactive and taking reasonable steps to prevent and correct complaints of sexual harassment, these policies may help to limit an employer's liability if complaints do occur.

REVIEW QUESTIONS

1. A sexual harassment policy and a non-fraternization policy both deal with illegal (unwelcome) behavior in the workplace.
2. The assertive person feels a need to control others.
3. Gender discrimination is a global concern.
4. Favoritism based on a consensual romantic relationship is illegal.
5. To reduce discrimination against women, employers should place value on characteristics traditionally associated with women.
6. Employees involved in workplace romances tend to experience poor work performance.
7. Male and female supervisors tend to have similar leadership styles.
8. Identify 3 major factors that have contributed to more women entering the workforce in the last 40 years.
9. Sexual harassment is a violation of Title VII of the 1964 Civil Rights Act.
10. Women are a minority group.

LEARNING ACTIVITIES

1. Divide the class into teams and have each team identify the advantages/ disadvantages of stereotyped gender characteristics.
2. Have a class discussion to identify the contributions or changes that have resulted from more women entering the workplace.

Issue Five

Cultural Values and Communication

"Different cultural values are good for different cultures"

Issue Five focuses on an important diversity concern that supervisors need to be aware of if they are going to understand and manage people from different cultures, cultural values. Understanding a person's value system is fundamental to understanding that person. Why people think and behave the way they do is influenced by their cultural conditioning. Contrary to what many Americans believe, the American way of thinking and behaving is not how most of the rest of the world thinks and behaves. At the same time, supervisors need to recognize that employees from different cultures also have much in common with each other.

To understand employees from different cultures, supervisors must develop multicultural communication skills. Unfortunately, communication between people from different cultures can be difficult, not only because of language differences that exist, but also perceptual differences. However, the more we interact with people who we consider to be "different" the greater the opportunity for communication and understanding to develop.

AMERICAN VALUES ARE NOT THE NORM

Each of us views the world from our own perception and we often believe that everyone else views the world from the same point of view. This false belief or perception is known as the "Me Principle." Similarly, most Americans have been conditioned to believe that the American way of thinking or doing things is the best way or how most of the rest of the world thinks and behaves.

46

At the same time, many Americans believe that if people from other cultures are not thinking or behaving according to American values, then those people or cultures are wrong.

In reality, the U.S. represents less than 5 percent of the world's population, therefore, the American way of thinking and behaving is in the minority. Globalization and workforce diversity have increased the degree of interaction taking place between people from different cultures. As a result, this has helped American businesses to recognize the benefits of other thinking styles and approaches to solving problems. Consequently, to effectively interact with and understand people from other cultures, we must be aware of the fact that most people in the world think and behave differently than how most Americans do.

To promote intercultural understanding, and reduce prejudice and discrimination, we need to examine some of the major components of culture and compare Americans cultural values with those of non-English speaking cultures.

Personal Space

The preference for the amount of physical space between people during interpersonal interactions is determined by culture. There are cultural standards which determine how close we should physically stand or sit next to others when interacting with them. A violation of these standards can make people feel uncomfortable and hinder relationship development.

For example, compared to many non-English speaking cultures, Americans prefer to have greater physical distance or space between themselves and others during most casual interactions and are offended or feel threatened when that distance is violated. This is especially true for many American males. People in our culture tend to be more territorial and have a strong desire for private space, preferring our own office, bedroom and fenced yard. However, for most people of non-English speaking cultures, casual interactions between them occur at closer physical distances.

Communication

Communicating across cultures is difficult, not only due to language differences, but also because of different cultural values. Culture determines how words are interpreted and influences how direct or indirect a person will be when communicating with others. Although certain words are shared by different cultures and may have the same spellings and pronunciations, their meanings may differ from one culture to another. For example, American English is different from the English spoken in Great Britain, Australia, and

Canada. Mexican Spanish is different from the Spanish spoken in Puerto Rico, Columbia and Spain. Consequently, although people from different cultures may speak the same language, cultural difference may make understanding difficult.

Another communication distinction has to do with how direct or indirect people from different cultures are with one another. Americans tend to be more direct when expressing their feelings and opinions compared to people of non-English speaking cultures. For example, a common expression used in our culture is that "the shortest distance between two points is a straight line." Meaning that we like to get to the main point or issue of a given problem or subject as soon as possible. On the other hand, people from many non-English speaking cultures use the following expression, "the shortest distance between two points is a curve." In other words, the interacting parties would prefer to first get acquainted with each another on an interpersonal level, and will eventually get to the main issue of a subject in a roundabout or indirect way.

Food and Eating Habits

Culture determines what, when and how we eat. Unfortunately, some misinformed Americans believe that the greatest benefit of our cultural and ethnic diversity is the variety of foods that are available in the U.S. Nevertheless, American employers need to be aware of different cultural food restrictions and taboos when sponsoring activities or functions that will involve the providing of food to employees from different cultures. For example:

- Jewish: prefer kosher foods, and avoid pork and shellfish
- Muslims: avoid pork and shellfish
- Hindus: avoid meat
- Vegetarians: avoid meat

Just as food preferences vary from one culture to another, so does food etiquette. What may be inappropriate or offensive table manners in one culture may be acceptable in another. For example, in some cultures, it is acceptable for everyone at the table to eat out of a common bowl of food using their hands instead of eating utensils, speak with their mouths full of food, and burp and lick their fingers while at the dinner table.

Sense of Time

Cultural differences exist on how time is viewed and used. Culture determines whether one is late, early or on time for a given event. For example,

Americans tend to be clock-oriented, which is in contrast with many non-English speaking cultures. Most Americans view time as finite and linear, meaning that they believe that there are time limits for accomplishing a given task and that eventually time runs out. For example, for most Americans time regulates our daily activities to the points where we often feel hurried, stressed and exhausted. In contrast, people of many non-English speaking cultures tend to view time as elastic and relative. For example, in many non-English speaking cultures, people prefer to perform their daily activities in a more relaxed and unhurried fashion, believing that tomorrow will always be available for completing a task.

Also, the traditional American approach to doing things involves the starting and finishing of one task at a time, while many non-English speaking cultures prefer doing many tasks simultaneously. It is important to realize that no culture has the best approach for using time or getting things done, only a different approach, with both advantages and disadvantages.

Dress and Appearance

There are different cultural standards that determine what is appropriate dress and appearance. For example, American culture tends to encourage individualism in many respects, including appearance. Americans also tend to make judgments about people based on appearance. Whether we are perceived to be likeable, trustworthy, financially well off, moral, or friendly is influenced by our clothing and overall appearance. Various hair styles, designer clothes, body fragrances, jewelry and tattoos are used to distinguish or define one American from another. On the other hand, people from many non-English speaking cultures are encouraged to dress similarly in order blend in or appear non-conspicuous.

Competition versus Cooperation

American culture tends to promote competition and individual rewards. As children, we were conditioned to believe in the value of competing and winning. Anytime we competed and won, we were rewarded in various ways, with recognition, status, trophies or money. Many aspects of American life are influenced by competition, such as business, sports, politics, and personal and work relationships.

On the other hand, people from many non-English speaking cultures have been encouraged to cooperate and value group rewards. At an early age, they were conditioned to work together and cooperate. While independence is promoted in American culture, interdependence is valued in many non-English speaking cultures.

Table 5.1.   Contrasting work characteristics of the U.S. with those of other cultures

U.S. characteristics	Characteristics of other cultures
short term employment opportunities	long term employment opportunities
individual responsibility	group responsibility
individual decision making	group decision making
specialized skills & careers	multi-skilled employee
work related employee concern	total person employee concern

Work Habits and Practices

Culture is a major influence in the workplace when considering workplace beliefs, behaviors, and business policies and practices. There are differences between traditional U.S. work beliefs, practices and policies compared to those of many non-English speaking industrial cultures as illustrated by Table 5.1.

It's interesting to note that globalization is creating more interaction between people from different cultures and as a result, traditional culture values are being influenced by those of other cultures. Consequently, intercultural interaction tends to create opportunities for exchanging ideas and learning from each other.

MULTICULTURAL COMMUNICATION

Because almost everything a supervisor does involves some form of communication, effective communication is necessary for supervisory success. In most organizations, supervisors spend over 80% of their time on the job communicating with employees in one form or another. Consequently, supervision is essentially a communication process since there are few activities a supervisor performs without using the communication process.

Unfortunately, there are communication barriers that need to be overcome in order to promote understanding, even among native English speaking employees. At the same time, when communicating with non-native English speaking employees, there are additional barriers that make understanding difficult. When interacting with employees from different cultures, language barriers and cultural values must be taken into consideration in order to promote understanding. The ability to effectively communicate with others requires that words have the same meanings. However, the meaning of words is determined by a person's culture.

Therefore, even if two people speak the same native language, they must also have similar cultural perceptions or "mind language" in order for words to have the same meanings and for understanding to occur. "Mind language" refers to a person's perceptions or ability to think as the other party in the conversation thinks. Our perceptions are based on our cultural backgrounds and experiences. Because people from the same culture have similar backgrounds and experiences, their perceptions are similar and therefore, the meanings of words used in conversation are the same. On the other hand, people from different cultures have different backgrounds and experiences and thus, the meanings for the same words used by two different cultures may be different, making it difficult for the parties to understand one another.

For example, people from the U.S. and Great Britain speak English. However, American English is different from the English spoken throughout Great Britain. Although most of the words used by both countries have the same spellings and pronunciations, the meanings of many of those words are different because of cultural differences, thus, making understanding between people of the U.S. and Great Britain more difficult than one might initially assume.

Because of the difficulties associated with intercultural communication, supervisors need to be aware of the following guidelines to improve communication with non-native English speaking employees.

Use Selective Vocabulary

Since most words have several meanings, it's important to choose words with the smallest range of meanings to promote understanding between people from different cultures. Most non-native English speakers are likely to know the first or second meanings of most English words. Therefore, when communicating with people from other cultures we need to focus on basic vocabulary and use words in their most common meaning.

Avoid Slang

Most American slang is difficult for people from other cultures to understand because slang tends to be cultural specific. Learning English as a second language often does not include the learning of American slang. Therefore, using slang can result in misunderstanding since the communicating parties have different perceptions due to their different cultural backgrounds and experiences.

Communicate in Several Ways

To promote understanding, we should communicate both verbally and nonverbally when interacting with people from different cultures. For example, signs, pictures, charts, and diagrams can be useful communication tools since they tend to have universal understanding. However, we need to use caution when using certain non-verbal communication signals, such as gestures, posture, and even silence. Just as the meaning of words is culturally determined, so are the meanings of nonverbal communication signals.

Speak at a Slower Rate

We need to exercise control over our rate of speech when communicating with non-native English speakers. We should slow our rate of speech when speaking to employees from different cultures since most non-native English speakers require more time to process and understand what is being said. Also, by speaking slower, we will be better able to be selective in our vocabulary and avoid slurring our words.

Exercise Care with Humor

What is humorous is subjective and varies from one person to another. When people from different cultures are involved, humor tends to be even more subjective and culturally based. Consequently, when using humor and jokes, we should exercise care since their understanding requires similar cultural perceptions, backgrounds and experiences. If the humor or jokes are not understood, non-native English speakers may interpret them as disrespectful comments and assume any laughing is being directed at them.

Expect a Delayed Reaction

We need to be patient when we are expecting a response from an employee who speaks English as a second language. It generally takes more time for non-native English speakers to translate what they have heard into their own language, and therefore, give a response back in English.

Perceptions Vary

Some Americans find it difficult to imagine that the typical American perception is not universal. In reality, how people think and behave is a reflection of their cultural experiences and values. Therefore, we may have to take more time to explain things in different ways to ensure that information conveyed to non-native English speakers is being understood.

Use Their Language

This is especially true when we first meet or interact with employees from different cultures. Using their language will create a positive first impression by indicating respect and a sincere desire to communicate with those employees. It can also encourage the learning of each other's language and promote understanding.

Provide a Question and Answer Session

Employees from different cultures may believe that it is inappropriate and impolite to interrupt or ask questions during group information and training sessions. Therefore, to promote understanding about anything that was said, supervisors should schedule a question and answer session during breaks or after a presentation.

Use Multicultural Trainers and Speakers

Non-native English speakers are better able to understand other non-native English speakers than native English speakers. Native English speakers tend to be more difficult to understand since they typically speak at a faster rate, slur their words and use slang more often. Therefore, when planning training sessions and presentations, include non-native English speaking trainers.

Communication is fundamental to relationship development and teamwork. Therefore, supervisors must exercise care when communicating with employees who speak English as a second language.

THE ISSUE OF LANGUAGE

The omnipresent effects of globalization have increased the frequency of interaction and degree of interdependence between nations and diverse people forcing more Americans and the business community to have to deal with diversity issues. Therefore, success for American businesses is contingent on the abilities of managers and employees to communicate, understand, and work with people having diverse backgrounds and cultures on an organizational, national and international level. In order to become effective leaders of business organizations and the global community, Americans will need to learn how to communicate and interact with people who are different or perceived to be different. Consequently, the ability to communicate with people from other cultures is of paramount concern and cannot be overstated.

Language is an important part of every culture and an essential component for communication. The ability to communicate with people from different cultures requires an understanding of the native languages of those cultures. Although two-thirds of the world is bilingual, learning a second language has not been encouraged in the U.S. as it has in most countries. In the long term, this inclination can have adverse consequences for American businesses. Unfortunately, some Americans are adamant about learning other languages and believe knowing a second language is not of much value. This is especially regrettable given the degree of diversity and number of bilingual people who live in the U.S., and as a result, the opportunities for learning a second language.

Opposition to learning a second language by Americans is reflected by the fact that over 30 states have passed laws designating English as the official language of those states. Also, some employers have attempted to establish "English-only workplace rules" to encourage their employees to speak English while in the workplace. The majority of courts that have considered the legality of "English-only workplace rules" have stated that requiring that English be spoken "at all times" while in the workplace is illegal because it results in national origin harassment and discrimination.

However, it is legal for employers to require that English be spoken "at certain times" while in the workplace if there is a legitimate business purpose or reason. Examples of business purpose where speaking English can be required at certain times while in the workplace include:

- while employees are performing their job duties
- for safety concerns
- for customer service reasons
- quality reasons, and
- during other work related periods

Aside from the legal concerns involved with "English-only workplace rules," there are benefits to employers and employees that knowing a second language may provide.

Benefits of Knowing a Second Language

Job Opportunities

Knowing a second language can enhance job opportunities in the global economy. Since the majority of jobs in the U.S. are in the service sector of the economy, this reflects the need for skills that are people-oriented and can be used to promote customer service. Having employees who are bilingual can help companies that are providing services and selling products, not only to Americans with different cultural backgrounds, but to people throughout the world. Also, supervisors who can communicate with employees of different cultures are more marketable than those who cannot. As globalization continues, the need to learn other languages will become an increasing business concern.

Additional Perspective

People from other cultures have different values and experiences, and as a result, perceive the world in different ways compared to traditional American perceptions. Therefore, knowing another language and having the opportunity to interact with people from other cultures can provide an additional perspective or way of thinking about life situations. Interaction between employees from different cultures promotes the exchange of ideas, experiences and knowledge, resulting in both parties learning from each other. Being able to look at the world in a different way allows us to better interpret situations and gives us more choices in deciding how to respond. For any given situation, the more options we have to choose from, the better our ultimate decision will be. By learning another language, we can gain insight into another way of viewing the world and events surrounding us.

Understanding Other People

Being bilingual contributes to improved understanding and interpersonal relationships between people from different cultures. Interaction between people of different cultures promotes an awareness of various cultural values, experiences and perspectives. Bilingual people have a communication advantage in social and work-related situations when interacting with people from other cultures. There is no equivalent substitute for direct interpersonal communication when trying to promote relationships and understanding about what is being said between two people. The degree of diversity that exists in the American workplace provides bilingual supervisors and employees with opportunities for effective communication and understanding of employees from different cultural backgrounds.

Communication Flexibility

Being bilingual can improve our vocabulary and communication skills in general. Knowing a second language can facilitate interpersonal communication by providing us with a greater range of vocabulary, and flexibility in communicating and expressing ourselves. The ability to get along with others requires that we exercise flexibility in our communicative style in order to enhance understanding. Communication flexibility also creates more opportunities for interaction. Because many English words are borrowed from other cultures or have their origin in other languages, understanding another language can provide us with alternative ways of expressing ourselves in different situations.

Better Understanding of Ourselves

While communicating and attempting to understand people from other cultures, we may gain a better understanding of ourselves. The opportunity to communicate with different people who have diverse cultures, backgrounds, experiences and viewpoints may cause us to reflect and question our beliefs and behaviors. As a result, the ability to communicate with people who have different perceptions may cause us to view ourselves in a different light, raise self awareness and motivate us to change our behavior or beliefs. Often, self awareness is a prerequisite to understanding ourselves and inspiring self improvement.

The opportunities for learning a second language in the U.S and the benefits that can be derived from a second language should encourage more Americans to become bilingual. There are no disadvantages from learning another language, only benefits. American must not become complacent by believing that future business opportunities can be realized by simply knowing English. As the globalization process continues, learning other languages will enhance individual success and organizational competitiveness.

REVIEW QUESTIONS

1. The meaning of most words is determined by culture.
2. Being a "risk-taker" is a major characteristic of non-English speaking cultures?
3. Which culture has the following belief, "the shortest distance between two points is a straight line?"
4. When speaking with a non-native English speaker, we should speak louder.
5. Approximately, one-third of the world's population is bilingual.
6. What are "Argots?"
7. What is "nepotism?"
8. How can we reduce Ethnocentrism?
9. What is the "Me Principle?"
10. Which culture of the world tends to have a low regard for authority?

LEARNING ACTIVITIES

1. Divide the class into teams and have each team identify the advantages or disadvantages of different cultural values.
2. Have a class discussion about the how American cultural values have changed within the last several years and the impact these changes have had on the workplace.

Issue Six

Disabilities and the Workplace

"There is diversity among people with the same disability"

Issue Six deals with one of the complex and misunderstood areas of diversity, managing employees with disabilities. Interacting, working and supervising employees with disabilities have become major concerns for employers and supervisors because of the fear and misunderstanding about disabilities in general and the law governing disabilities. To effectively supervise employees with disabilities, supervisors need to have a general understanding of the Americans With Disabilities Act of 1990.

Unfortunately, one of the major obstacles people with disabilities encounter as applicants and employees are the negative fears, stereotypes and misconceptions about disabilities. As a result, people with disabilities often become victims of discrimination. Fortunately, as more people with disabilities enter the workplace and more education about disabilities is disseminated, more opportunities for interaction and understanding will take place. This will help to alleviate some of the concerns about people with disabilities.

SUPERVISING EMPLOYEES WITH DISABILITIES

There is much uncertainty and even fear by employers and supervisors over how to supervise employees with disabilities. Part of the confusion is due to the lack of experience in supervising employees with disabilities and understanding on what is required by the principal federal law dealing with disabilities, the Americans With Disabilities Act of 1990. Other reasons for confusion are due to false stereotypes and the lack of information about employees who have disabilities.

For the most part, supervisors should supervise employees with protected disabilities in the same way they supervise employees without disabilities. Employees with disabilities should be held to the same performance, attendance and behavior standards that all other employees are held to. To do otherwise would constitute reverse discrimination against those employees who don't have protected disability. The only difference when dealing with employees with disabilities is that employers must provide "reasonable accommodations" for employees with disabilities to enable them to perform the "essential functions" of their jobs. Essential functions refer to the basic job duties of a particular job. A reasonable accommodation requires the employers to make changes in the workplace or a particular job to enable the employee with a disability to perform the essential functions of the job. However, reasonable accommodations do not require employers to:

- create a new position for an employee with a disability
- reassign or transfer other employees to accommodate an employee with a disability
- promote an employee with a disability to a new position
- violate a collective bargaining agreement, or

When interacting with employees who are "different" or perceived to be different, sometimes supervisors forget to use common sense and basic human relations skills. Employees with disabilities have similar desires, interests and career goals as do employees who don't have protected disabilities. As is true for most people we initially perceive as being "different," once we get to know them, we often realize that we have more in common with each other than differences.

Basic Guidelines When Interacting With Employees With Disabilities

Wheelchairs

When interacting with employees in wheelchairs, sit down when conversations are going to be longer than a minute and don't casually touch or lean on someone's wheelchair. Americans tend to be territorial about their personal space and wheelchairs are considered to be personal space that should not be violated by a casual acquaintance.

Visual Impairments

When dealing with employees who have visual impairments, don't speak louder than normal, and don't be afraid to use words such as see, look, or blind. Also, don't distract a guide dog, if present, from its functions by playing with it or feeding it.

Hearing Impairments

When dealing with employees who have hearing impairments consider providing information in writing and encourage employees to ask questions for clarification. Also avoid speaking unusually fast.

General Guidelines

It's important to realize that employees with disabilities are not all the same. Also, there is diversity among employees having the same disabilities. In other words, the severity and nature of a disability varies from one person to another, along with the ability of each person to deal with a particular disability. Consequently, employees who have the same disabilities may require different accommodations, depending on the severity of a given disability and the individual involved. At the same time, we cannot assume all employees with disabilities are the same and need special assistance or the same accommodation.

When communicating with employees who have disabilities, we should maintain eye contact and encourage questions for clarification, just as we would with any employee. Incidentally, most of the guidelines suggested above can easily apply to people who don't have visible disabilities. Also, the term "disability" should be used instead of "handicapped."

It's important that supervisors learn how to control or manage their thinking about employees who are perceived as "different."

Guidelines for Managing Our Thinking About Differences

Change Attitudes

First, we need to recognize that the attitudes we have about people will either consciously or subconsciously influence how we treat them. How a supervisor treats his/her employees will influences their behavior and performance. Therefore, the supervisor's attitude about an employee can play a critical role in how successful that employee becomes. Fortunately, we are not born with certain attitudes about people. Instead, the attitudes we have about people are learned, including those attitudes about people with disabilities. Consequently, we can change our attitudes by consciously unlearning or discarding old attitudes and learning new ones.

Be Curious

Be curious about people who we perceive as being "different." When dealing with diverse people in general, we should maintain an open mind. Look beyond their perceived differences or disabilities, and view each interaction as a potential learning experience. By not focusing on a person's disability, we may come to realize that we have more in common with them than is different.

Use "What If" Questions

We need to ask ourselves "What If" questions. "What if" questions are a good way to promote understanding because they allow us to simulate different possibilities and prepare us for future scenarios. For example, we can ask ourselves, "what if" we or a family member develops a disability or "what if" we or a family member has a "significant other" who is perceived to be "different." "What if" questions allows us the opportunity to view our beliefs and behavior in an objective light and at the same time, sensitize us to different life situations that may be beyond a person's ability to control.

We Will Become "Them"

Recognize that the way we treat others may later be reciprocated upon us. In other words, we need to realize that we are not always going to be young, attractive and without disabilities. In time we will become one of "them," a person who is perceived as being "different," and therefore, we will most likely experience negative stereotyping, prejudice and employment discrimination. Unfortunately, everyone has the potential for being in a legally protected group, either because we will eventually be 40 years old or develop a legally recognized and protected disability.

Employees with disabilities are not any different from those who don't have recognized disabilities. Likewise, interacting or supervising employees with disabilities does not have to be a difficult or fearful experience. Instead, we must remember that people with disabilities are people first, who just happen to have a disability or different challenge than we have.

THE AMERICANS WITH DISABILITIES ACT

The Americans With Disabilities Act (ADA) was signed into law in 1990, however, Title I of the act, the title dealing with employment discrimination, didn't take effect until July 26, 1992. The reason for the two year delay was that Congress wanted to give the business community time to adjust to the new law. Title I is one of several titles to the ADA which are designed to prohibit discrimination against people with disabilities in various aspects of society. In addition to the title dealing with employment discrimination, there are titles prohibiting discrimination in public accommodations, public transportation, and telecommunication services. Title I imposes two duties on employers:

1. Employers are prohibited from discriminating against qualified individuals with disabilities in employment, and
2. Employers are required to make reasonable accommodations for an employee's disability as long as those accommodations do not impose an undue hardship on the employer

To understand Title I, we need to examine the individual components of each duty. Title I of the ADA prohibits discrimination in employment against qualified individuals with disabilities in hiring, placement, promotion, wages, benefits and other terms, conditions and privileges of employment. The ADA has three definitions of a "person with a disability." According to the ADA, a "person with a disability" is any person:

(1) with a mental or physical impairment which substantially limits a major life activity, such as the ability to work,
(2) who has a record of such an impairment, or
(3) who is perceived as having such an impairment

A "qualified person" with a disability is a person who (a) satisfies the job specifications for the job in question, and (b) can perform the "essential functions" of that job with or without "reasonable accommodations." Job specifications refer to the human qualifications an employee needs to have to perform a specific job, such as having the requisite education, experience and skills. Essential job functions refer to the basic duties of a job, such as the tasks, responsibilities and duties the need to be performed.

The ADA requires that employers make "reasonable accommodations" for an employee with a disability, as long as those accommodations do not impose an "undue hardship" on the business. Reasonable accommodations refers to making changes to the workplace or job itself in order to enable the employee with the disability to perform the essential job functions. Examples of "reasonable accommodations" include:

- make the workplace accessible to persons with disabilities
- job restructuring, job sharing or job reassignment
- equipment and furniture modifications
- part-time and modified work schedules
- a reserved parking space
- leave of absence

Undue hardship is defined as any accommodation imposing "significant" expense or difficulty on the business. Significant expense or difficulty varies among organizations and is determined on a case by case basis. In other words, what may be a significant expense for one organization may not be for another due to differences in the financial resources available.

Although the ADA requires employers to make some adjustments in the workplace, for most employers, complying with the ADA will not be difficult or expensive. Most issues that arise from complying with the ADA can be resolved through communication and the use of common sense. Through an "interactive" process or dialogue between the employer and the employee with the disability, the parties can have an opportunity to exchange information with each other and increase the probability of identifying a mutually agreed upon accommodation.

Suggestions to help employers comply with the ADA requirement of reasonable accommodations include:

- make the workplace accessible to people with disabilities
- review job descriptions to determine the "essential functions" required for each position
- during interviews, ask only job related questions
- don't test for disabilities, instead, test for the skills and abilities required for the specific job
- base all employment decisions on the ability to perform the "essential functions" of the job
- examine attitudes about people with disabilities and refrain from making employment decisions based on negative myths, fear or stereotypes about them

Globalization and a shortage of skilled labor are forcing American organizations to efficiently use every available source of human capital. Consequently, as is true with any minority group, people with disabilities represent a largely untapped resource with unlimited potential and can provide major benefits for employers. Whether employers like it or not, the ADA is the law and establishes minimum standards to protect the rights of people with disabilities. It's important for employers to provide training to supervisors and employees about the requirements of the ADA to promote understanding and ensure that the organization is in compliance.

PERSONAL COMFORT ZONES

Sometimes when we first meet someone, we like them immediately while on other occasions and for no apparent reason, we may take an instant dislike to someone we meet for the first time. Think about the last time you met someone you liked or disliked and why you felt the way you did? What were the factors that contributed to how you felt about someone you just met? Often, whether we like or dislike someone is influenced by how comfortable we feel when we are around them. How relaxed and comfortable we feel when interacting with someone is dependent on a number of factors. Unfortunately, sometimes we allow certain factors, such as race, gender or ethnicity, that are beyond a person's ability to control to overly influence how we think, feel and behave toward people.

Most of us develop certain "comfort zones" or "comfort levels" with certain individuals or groups of people, which are influenced by gender, race, ethnicity, age, disabilities and other characteristics that are often outside that person's ability to control or change. Sometimes, our thoughts and behavior toward others occur without conscious awareness. It's as though our thinking and behavior are the result of an unconscious, automatic response mechanism that we cannot control and may not even be aware of.

How comfortable we feel when we are with someone influences how we treat them and can affect the development of the relationship. From a supervisory standpoint, a supervisor's comfort level toward his employees will influence how he/she treats, evaluates and communicates with them. Consequently, how that employee is treated will influence his/her behavior, performance and success within the organization.

People that we feel comfortable with are treated favorably, while people we don't feel comfortable with are treated less favorably and discriminated against. Generally speaking, we tend to be more comfortable around people who we perceive to be similar to us. Our comfort level is highest among people who have a similar background, culture and appearance as we do. Because of the similarities with us, we tend to view and treat them favorably. On the other hand, people who we perceive as different from us are viewed and treated less favorably.

For example, some people are least comfortable interacting with individuals from certain ethnic groups, while others are least comfortable around people from different generations or people who have certain types of disabilities. This lack of comfort influences our behavior toward them and our willingness to interact with them on a social or work-related basis. As a result, we tend to avoid interacting with them by choosing not to hire them or if they are currently working in our company, we attempt to avoid having to work with them and don't socialize with them outside the job. On the other hand, people we are comfortable with, we choose to hire and socialize with them, both inside and outside the workplace.

Much of how we think and feel about certain groups is the result of the learning process. Prejudice and our behavior towards different groups are learned, either from personal experience with members of certain groups or indirectly from our family, relatives and friends when we were children. Our early life experiences have left their impact on us and continue to influence our comfort level with people of certain groups when we become adults.

However, because prejudice is a learned attitude, it can be unlearned or changed. Often, the initial step in dealing with any problem is to become aware of the problem. Awareness of how we think, feel and behave toward individuals of certain groups can help us in controlling our thoughts and behavior toward them. Therefore, to improve our comfort zone we need to be aware and take responsibility of our prejudices toward people who are different. Then, we can learn new ways of thinking about people who are different by taking control of our thoughts and choosing to think differently about them. Experience in interacting with people who we perceive to be different, and being open to learning new things from others can promote positive thoughts about people. Prejudice can be reduced and our comfort levels with individuals of different groups improved by being consciously aware of our prejudices and controlling our thinking about them.

Some companies have attempted to improve the comfort levels and therefore the working relationships between employees of different races, genders and cultures through various education and training programs, such as with diversity training. Being sensitive to the feelings of others and learning about different cultural values are major components of the training. Diversity training can also promote better interpersonal and work relationships by helping employees to recognize their prejudices toward certain groups and develop strategies for overcoming them. For example, prejudice and discrimination can be reduced by identifying the benefits that differences among people can provide and recognizing that despite our differences we have many things in common with each other.

As is true with any type of learning, it takes time to unlearn old attitudes and behaviors and learn new ones. Unfortunately, the learning process is gradual and learning new attitudes and behaviors requires practice and patience. At the same time, we must remember that whatever attitudes and behaviors we have did not develop overnight, but overtime. Consequently, with time and a desire to change, positive attitudes and behaviors toward people who are different can be learned and relationship development can be promoted.

REVIEW QUESTIONS

1. The interview is the best forum to ask job applicants if they have any disabilities.
2. What is meant by a "reasonable accommodation" under the ADA?
3. What is the difference between a job description and a job specification?
4. When speaking with a blind or visually-impaired person, we need to speak louder.
5. A person who is an alcoholic is protected from employment discrimination by the ADA.
6. At any point in time anyone of us can become a person with a disability.
7. What is meant by "essential job functions" under the ADA?
8. Most of us have "comfort zones" related to people who are "different."
9. Negative stereotypes are major barriers that people with disabilities encounter in society and the workplace.
10. The ADA requires affirmative action by employers in the private employment sector.

LEARNING ACTIVITIES

1. Divide the class into teams and have each team develop guidelines for dealing with people having different types of disabilities.
2. Have a class discussion where students identify experiences and concerns they have had when interacting with people with disabilities and how they dealt with those concerns.

Recruiting for a Diverse Workforce

"The use of objective and job related hiring criteria ensures fairness"

Issue Seven deals with the important and time consuming process of recruiting and hiring diversity. For most organizations, managing diversity begins with the recruiting and hiring process. However, traditional strategies for recruiting employees may need to be supplemented in order to ensure that an adequate pool of diverse and qualified applicants is available. Job descriptions and specifications need to be up-to-date in order to facilitate the hiring process.

Unfortunately, sometimes the best qualified person for a job is not hired because of discrimination based on stereotypes and prejudice, or an inaccurate selection process. Consequently, hiring and promotion decisions often have legal implications that supervisors need to be aware of to avoid complaints and lawsuits. Using objective and job related selection criteria, and understanding the pertinent diversity related laws are prerequisites for ensuring that the best qualified employees are hired.

EMPLOYERS SHOULD EXERCISE CARE WHEN HIRING

Due to the expense, time and potential liability involved, hiring new employees can be one of the most difficult and yet important tasks an employer has to perform. It's an important task because organizational efficiency is dependent on the performance of the employees, such that if the employees are high performers then there's a higher probability for organizational success and vice versa. It's a difficult task because trying to identify the best qualified person for a job is not an exact science since the hiring process can have potential shortcomings. In either case, in today's competitive economy, every hiring decision is critical to an organization's success.

When evaluating the skills, work experience and education of job applicants, another concern confronting employers is the increasing amount of resume fraud and applicant dishonesty taking place. Competition for jobs has created a climate where applicants will lie, cheat and deceive to get a good job, or feel compelled to omit and conceal negative information about themselves. For example, some applicants may falsify or exaggerate their qualifications and experience, and attempt to conceal criminal records or reasons for leaving previous jobs.

Also, in today's litigious society, lawsuits based on negligent hiring are becoming more common. Especially when employers fail to exercise reasonable care when evaluating and investigating job applicants who subsequently harm others while on the job. For example, hiring a convicted child molester as a day care assistant, a convicted thief as a bank guard or a heavy machine operator with a history of incompetence may result in negligent hiring lawsuits if someone is hurt or incurs a loss due to a failure to exercise reasonable care when making hiring decisions.

The best way to avoid future problems with an employee is to make sure the best qualified person is hired in the first place. Unfortunately, many employers want to spend as little time as possible hiring new employees, feeling that their time could be better spent elsewhere. However, if employers don't spend a reasonable amount of time when deciding who to hire, they may hire the wrong employees and thus create future problems for themselves and the organization. It is therefore in the best interest of every employer to properly evaluate and conduct thorough background investigations on all applicants prior to hiring them.

Employers need to understand that every employee hired is an investment for the organization. The organization is going to invest time and money orienting and training newly hired employees. If a hiring decision ends up being a mistake, not only will the organization experience performance or behavior problems and lose out on its hiring and training investment, but lawsuits of wrongful discharge or negligent hiring may result. Also, the organization is going to have to spend time and money to initiate another search and screening process to fill the vacancy that occurred.

Finally, employers must ensure that the hiring process is in compliance with equal employment opportunity laws and regulations to limit complaints of discrimination. It doesn't cost a rejected job applicant any money to file a discrimination complaint with the federal Equal Employment Opportunity Commission (EEOC) or, a similar state or municipal agency. Consequently, employers must avoid making hiring decisions based on an applicant's race, color, religion, national origin, gender, disability or age.

Some additional applicant characteristics that employers may want to remain neutral or exercise care about when making hiring decisions include the following.

- Arrest record: Title VII of the 1964 Civil Rights Act concerns (disparate impact theory). Certain minority groups have a higher incidence of arrest and therefore, basing an employment decision solely on arrest record may have an adverse impact on a protected group. Also, it must be remembered that an arrest is not a conviction.
- Facial hair: Title VII concerns (disparate impact theory). Certain religious beliefs require that men maintain facial hair. Consequently, basing employment decisions on the fact that someone has facial hair may be perceived as discrimination based on religion.
- Height & weight: Title VII concerns (disparate impact theory). Having height or weight standards as a job criterion may create an adverse impact on certain minority groups and women and therefore, may be illegal if those criteria are not job related.
- Accents & language: Title VII concerns (disparate impact theory). Refusing to hire someone because they have an accent or speak English as a second language may constitute national origin discrimination.
- Alcoholism & drug addiction: The Americans With Disabilities Act concerns. Alcoholism and drug addition are considered to be protected disabilities and therefore, basing employment decisions on such disabilities is illegal. At the same time, employers can enforce rules against employees using alcohol or drugs on the job. In other words, testing for drugs in the workplace is legal. The ADA only protects "recovering" alcoholics and drug addicts from employment discrimination.
- Citizenship status: Immigration Reform & Control Act concerns. Employer must refrain from discriminating against non-U.S. citizens who have the legal right to work in the U.S.

The best way to ensure that the anti-discrimination laws are not being violated is to base all employment decisions, including the decisions to hire, on objective and job related criteria.

MAKING THE HIRING PROCESS MORE EFFECTIVE

Hiring decisions play a critical role in an organization's success. High performing employees can help to make the supervisor's job easier and promote a high performing organization. Therefore, the right hiring decision can result in an employee who will compliment the organization and help it to achieve its goals, while the wrong decision can have the opposite results. Although the hiring process may have certain limitations, because you can never be certain that the best qualified person was hired, there are several steps employers can take to make it more effective.

First, employers need to document the entire hiring process to create a record and preserve evidence of nondiscrimination, in case decisions are challenged. Today, dissatisfied applicants are more educated about the law and have become more creative in challenging hiring decisions. At the same time, they have greater access to the courts and various governmental employment agencies, such as the Equal Employment Opportunity Commission, for filing complaints of discrimination. Discrimination complaints are not only costly and time consuming for employers to defend, they can also generate negative publicity and have an adverse effect on organizational performance and morale.

To fill any job vacancy, employers need to determine the job description and job specifications for that position. A job description identifies major job functions, such as the duties, responsibilities and tasks that need to be performed. It's important for each job description to be current to ensure accuracy and to identify the "essential functions" of every position in order to meet the requirements of the Americans With Disabilities Act of 1990. Job specifications identify the minimum qualifications necessary to perform a given job, such as the education, skills and work experience needed. Employers should avoid establishing job specifications that are unnecessarily greater than what is necessary to adequately perform the job. High qualifications will generally require that a higher salary be offered and may also violate equal employment opportunity laws if a large percentage of women and minority applicants are screened out resulting in an adverse impact.

Employers need to have a consistent policy for accepting and reviewing applications. Inconsistency can create confusion and the perception of unfairness, thus leading to complaints of discrimination. Applicants should be warned that supplying false information will result in a denial of employment. References, especially from the applicant's former supervisor, should be checked because they can provide valuable information about the applicant's job performance and work habits. References should be in writing and applicants should be warned that all references will be checked.

Having applicants sign or acknowledge a release form which gives their consent for background investigations is important, not only for the hiring employer, but to also gain the cooperation of former employers in disclosing relevant information about their former employees. Without such a release, many former employers will be reluctant to provide information about a former employee due to defamation and other litigation concerns. A background investigation should be undertaken to verify information submitted, screen out undesirable applicants and provide a defense if negligent hiring is alleged. To avoid liability if sued for negligent hiring, the employer must provide evidence of having exercised reasonable care when hiring an employee.

Because most employment relationships are based on the "at-will" employment doctrine, employers can generally hire whomever they wish, as long as the equal employment opportunity laws are not violated. Equal employment opportunity requires consistent and objective evaluations of all applicants to ensure nondiscrimination. Therefore, hiring decisions should be based on objective and job related criteria.

Interviews should be conducted in a consistent and objective manner to ensure equal treatment. Preparing a list of written questions in advance of the interview that are relevant to the qualifications necessary to perform the job will establish consistency and nondiscrimination since all applicants will be asked the same questions. Also, a comparison of each applicant's response to the same questions asked can be made.

One way to compare the qualifications of each applicant is through the use of a screening tool known as an "applicant evaluation checklist." Each applicant should be evaluated using this checklist which can ease the screening process and help ensure consistent treatment. An "applicant evaluation checklist" consists of a written list of job qualifications identified for a given position which can be used to evaluate or compare the qualifications of each applicant applying for the job. This checklist can establish a record of nondiscrimination and prove to be valuable if complaints of unequal treatment arise. The more checks and balances that exist in the hiring process the better.

The key to effective hiring is consistency of treatment and the use of objective and job related criteria. At the same time, hiring the best qualified person requires a time commitment by the employer. However, it is time well spent when a proper match is made between the job and the person hired. If a reasonable amount of time is not put into the hiring process and a poor choice is made, even more time will be required to correct that decision. It should be recognized that hiring decisions are some of the most important decisions supervisors will be involved with because they will have a direct impact on the current and future success of the organization.

RECRUITING FOR DIVERSITY

The shortage of employees with the requisite skills needed in today's economy has forced companies to compete with each other in order to find the best qualified employees available. The shortage of qualified employees, along with the recognized benefits associated with a diverse workforce, has encouraged many employers to develop strategies to locate, hire and promote diversity. Although diversity is everywhere, recruiting and hiring diverse employees have sometimes been difficult for some employers.

To attain a diverse workforce, most organizations will need to supplement traditional recruitment strategies with strategies specifically designed to locate, hire and promote diversity. As is true when attempting to fill any job vacancy, the first step in recruiting diversity is to consider where to look. The obvious places where employers can begin the search for diversity are either within or outside the organization. There are certain benefits that can be realized from recruiting, hiring and promoting from either within or outside the organization.

Within the Organization

Loyalty and Reduced Turnover

Filling vacancies and promoting from within the organization gives current employees an opportunity to advance and rewards them for their years of service and loyalty. Also, this may reduce job dissatisfaction and turnover, which are major problems and costs associated with the management of human resources.

Shorter Learning Curve

Promoting from within the organization usually results in a shorter orientation period, and reduces the amount of time required for employees to develop competency and experience in their new positions. Because an existing employee knows the systems, procedures and people within the organization, less time will be spent adjusting to the new position and the organization.

Less Expense

Promoting from within the organization generally involves less expense compared to going outside it to fill vacancies. Money and time that would normally be spent on advertising and bring in prospective employees from outside the organization would be saved.

Accurate & Reliable Information

The information an employer has on a current employee is based on past experience and performance evaluations of that employee and therefore, is generally more accurate and reliable. On the other hand, anytime an employee is hired from the outside, the company can never really be sure how qualified the person is until he/she is actually performing the job. That's because when an employee is hired from the outside, most of the information about the employee is provided by the applicant. Therefore that information may not be reliable or accurate, including the information provided by references. Also, competition for jobs has encouraged some applicants to embellish their qualifications and commit resume fraud.

Outside the Organization

Relevant Skills and Experience

Expanding the search for new employees to outside the organization is sometimes necessary because current employees may not have the relevant skills or experience needed for the vacant position. Rather then experiencing a prolonged decline in performance while waiting for a current employee to receive training and develop competency, the organization may be better off hiring from the outside.

Different Ideas and Experiences

Hiring from outside the organization can help to encourage the introduction of different ideas, knowledge, experiences and techniques. Too much inbreeding, where no new employees are hired or promoted from the outside, and thus no new ideas introduced, can be detrimental for an organization. On the other hand, when employees are hired from outside the organization, the knowledge and experiences of those newly hired employees can be combined with that of current employees, resulting in the entire organization benefiting from the shared information.

Best Qualified Person

The ultimate goal of the hiring process is to hire the best qualified person. Extending the search to include applicants from both inside and outside the organization can ensure that a thorough search will be made to find the best qualified person available. The more applicants an employer has to choose from, the greater the likelihood of hiring the best qualified person.

Recruiting Methods

Traditional Recruiting Methods

Locating diverse employees requires employers to use a variety of recruiting methods. However, employer must not overlook the obvious methods for recruiting employees. Table 7.1 lists recruiting methods traditionally used by organizations.

Table 7.1.   Traditional Recruiting Methods

local & national newspapers ads	specialized magazine ads
employee referrals	high schools
walk-ins	colleges and universities
job fairs	internships

Supplemental Recruiting Methods

Recruiting for diversity often requires employers to become more creative and supplement traditional recruitment methods. Table 7.2 lists supplemental recruiting methods organizations can use to recruit diversity.

Strategies for Hiring Diversity

Encouraging diverse employees to apply and accept employment offers with an organization may call for creative strategies designed to address some of the specific concerns of a diverse workforce. Employers need to be flexible and innovative if they are serious about hiring diversity. The traditional approaches for recruiting and hiring are not going to be effective with diversity.

Table 7.2.   Supplemental Recruiting Methods

email recruiting	temp agencies
employee finder's bonuses	reward departments for hiring diversity
diversity search committees	community organizations
professional search firms	diversity hiring as part of supervisor evaluation
full time diversity recruiters	governmental agencies
on-the-job training programs	promote company as "diversity friendly"
affirmative action	

Table 7.3. Diversity Related Concerns

diversity role models	mentorship programs
"good cause" discharge policy	job security incentives
flexible work schedules	cafeteria style employee benefit programs
signing incentives	child care services
buddy systems	company reputation as "diversity friendly"
career development opportunities	use of objective and job related evaluation criteria
cultural awareness activities	orientation programs for new employees

Therefore, employers should consider whether the concerns of diversity are being identified and properly addressed by the organization. Table 7.3 lists some of the important concerns employers need to address when recruiting diverse employees.

Recruiting for a diverse workforce does not have to be difficult. Overtime, most employers will discover that recruiting for diversity tends to be self generating once the process begins. In other words, as a company hires more diverse people, more diverse people tend to apply for jobs with the company. As is true when trying to achieve any goal, including workforce diversity, the most difficult part is getting started.

Closely related to recruitment and hiring, is employee retention. The efforts involved in recruitment and hiring diversity will be lost if those newly hired employees do not remain with the organization. Fortunately, many of the techniques identified for recruiting and hiring diversity can also be applied to retention. Consequently, the methods identified for recruiting and hiring diversity can be used to achieve multiple business goals.

As more members of the Baby Boomer Generation retire and the globalization process continues, the shortage of qualified employees will become incessantly critical. Therefore, American organizations will be forced to become more creative in their recruitment, hiring and retention strategies.

REVIEW QUESTIONS

1. What is an advantage of promoting from within the organization?
2. Why should objective and job related criteria be used to evaluate job applicants?
3. Traditional images of what an ideal employee should look like ought to be used when recruiting employees.
4. What type(s) of employment discrimination does Title VII of the 1964 Civil Rights Act prohibit?
5. Why should we exercise care when considering the arrest record of a job applicant?

6. What is an advantage of promoting from outside the organization?
7. Where is a good place to recruit for diversity?
8. How should E-mail resumes be treated?
9. How should we handle requests for information about former employees?
10. Why are background checks on job applicants important?

LEARNING ACTIVITIES

1. Have a class discussion on the pertinent equal employment opportunity laws that prohibit discrimination based on certain traits/characteristics.
2. Have a class discussion where students talk about some of their positive and negative experiences when job hunting.

Issue Eight

New Generations in the Workplace

"Understand and appreciate the values of each generation"

Issue Eight focuses on the changes taking place in the workplace and how values affect the management of different generations of employees. A person's value system determines what is important to that person. Since values influence how people think and behave, the supervisor's job has become more challenging because each generation of employees has different values that need to be understood for the effective management of diversity.

Supervisors and employees must recognize that today's business environment is more complex, competitive and dynamic than what it was ten years ago. One consequence is that employees need to become multi-skilled employees. Because technological change has become a permanent fixture in the workplace, organizational success is contingent on the abilities of supervisors and employees to be future oriented and prepared for the next paradigm shift.

MANAGING GENERATION X

The composition of the American labor force has undergone dramatic changes within the last 40 years. As a result, supervisors need to develop skills that will enable them to manage, not only women, minorities and people with disabilities, but also employees from different generations. Today, the job of the typical supervisor has become more challenging because he/she must be a multicultural and multigenerational leader to be effective. For example, one of the newer generations to enter the workforce in recent years are people born between 1964–1981. People in this generation, commonly

Table 8.2.   Other names for Generation X

13th Generation	Unknown Generation
Sesame Street Generation	Latch-key Generation
Generation E	GenXers

referred to as Generation X, will become one of the dominate groups of employees and leaders of business organizations in the future. Table 8.2 lists some of the various names that are used to refer to Generation X.

Every generation has different values and attitudes that impact their thinking and behavior. When comparing Generation X to previous generations of employees, it's important for supervisors to understand the distinctive characteristics of Generation X to effectively manage these employees.

Characteristics of Generation X

Less Regard for Authority

Generation X has less regard or fear of authority than previous generations of employees. Because they are more educated, Generation X employees are more likely to express their opinions and challenge authority. Therefore, to manage Generation X, supervisors will need to exercise flexible leadership and develop their interpersonal skills. Supervisors will realize that they will be more effective if they use their interpersonal skills when managing younger employees, as opposed to relying exclusively on authority.

Desire for Involvement in Decision-Making

Because Generation X is comprised of educated employees, they have higher expectations of what jobs should provide compared to previous generations of employees. Whereas previous generations of employees were most concerned with satisfying their lower level needs, such as receiving adequate pay, company benefits and safe working conditions, Generation X has a greater desire to satisfy their higher level needs. Higher level needs can be satisfied by meeting the psychological expectations of employees. As a result, younger employees not only want jobs that pay well, they also want jobs that are interesting, challenging and stimulating. They desire "empowerment," which is involvement in organizational decision-making, problem-solving and goal-setting.

Desire for Career Security

Because of the economic uncertainty confronting American organizations, most employers are not able to promise long term employment. Consequently, younger employees are less willing to "pay dues" or defer rewards as previous generations of employees did. As a result, younger employees have a greater desire for immediate recognition and feedback, are more self-reliant, and feel that long term employment depends on keeping their skills up-to-date. Since employers cannot promise job security, they will need to provide younger employees with short term rewards and opportunities for career development. The majority of younger employees want careers with prospects for advancement and not simply jobs.

Comfortable with Change and New Technology

Generation X grew up during the information and technology revolution, and as a result, is familiar and comfortable with change and new technology. E-mail, voice mail, fax machines, cellular phones and rapid technological innovations are a major part of this generation. The workplace of the future is going to be dominated by continual change and will require that employees have the ability to adapt to that change. Because the skills and information content of jobs are constantly changing, the adaptability and technological experience of Generation X are conducive with a dynamic workplace.

Desire for Independence

The early family related experiences of Generation X have influenced their work related expectations. As a product of the two income family, Generation X grew up with a large degree of independence, the responsibility of taking care of themselves, and the experience of making their own decisions. This conditioning has created a desire on the part of Generation X for empowerment, not only in their personal lives, but also in the workplace. Consequently, self managed work groups, indirect supervision, delegation and a desire for responsibility are important job attributes that will motivate Generation X.

Although Generation X is a relatively small generation comprised of approximately 50 million people, their impact on the workplace will be significant. The shortage of qualified employees is threatening the ability of American organizations to satisfy the needs of the global marketplace. Therefore, younger employees are going to play larger roles in ensuring the future success of business organizations. At the same time, organizations that fail to address the needs of Generation X will experience difficulty in motivating and retaining this valuable and talented source of labor.

MANAGING GENERATION Y

The newest and one of the largest generations to enter the American labor force is known as Generation Y. This generation is composed of people born between the end of the 1970s and the year 2000 (approximately 1979–2000). There are approximately 80 million people in this generation and it will eventually make up 27 percent of the U.S. labor force. In comparison with the preceding generations, Generation X is made up of approximately 50 million people and the Baby Boom Generation, approximately 76 million. As is true with any distinct group, Generation Y has certain characteristics which can be useful for supervisors to be aware of in order to effectively manage the employees of this generation.

Characteristics of Generation Y

Desire for Involvement in Decision Making

Involvement in various functions of the organization, including problems solving and decision making, are important for this generation. Generation Y has a desire to understand how their jobs and contributions are going to impact their future and the success of the organization. As holistic thinkers, they will want to know the rationale underlying any given management decision and are not afraid to ask questions in order to understand situations.

The desire for involvement has also made Generation Y more civic minded, resulting in a high rate of volunteerism, both inside and outside the workplace compared to Generation X. Therefore, community and organizational volunteerism are expected to continue as the careers of Generation Y progresses.

Desire for Career Opportunities

Training opportunities, learning experiences and other types of career development are vital concerns for this generation. At the same time, Generation Y has positive expectations about themselves and their futures. Some reasons for their optimism is that the global economy has provided them with more opportunities for continual education, different careers and various job options, compared with previous generations of employees.

Compensation based on merit and job performance is important to Generation Y. Conversely, seniority systems or across-the-board raises are not going to be effective motivators for this generation. Also, cafeteria type employee benefit plans, job enlargement, flexible work schedules and time away from the workplace are appealing job attributes.

Comfortable with Change and New Technology

Generation Y is the most technologically literate generation in American history. Consequently, they are highly adaptable to change and new technology. As their careers develop, Generation Y's technological expertise will continue to grow and influence their organization's efforts to meet new challenges in the global marketplace. Also, through teleconferencing, instant messaging, telecommuting, and other innovations, Generation Y will help make the virtual workplace the new reality.

Another change Generation Y will continue to deal with throughout their careers is diversity. However, compared to previous generations, Generation Y is more accepting of people who are different because of their early exposure to various diversity issues through the media, social interactions, classmates and travel. As a result, Generation Y will continue to play a positive role in influencing societal and workplace attitudes about diversity.

Multitask Oriented

In addition to their education and technological expertise, Generation Y has more broad based knowledge and work experience than previous generations. Consequently, their ideas can be valuable contributions to organizational success. Being the best educated generation, they will want to be involved in organizational decision making, problem solving and goal setting.

Generation Y has been conditioned to be more multitask oriented than previous generations. They have been able to develop skills that allow them to perform many tasks simultaneously without experiencing unhealthy stress. Also, Generation Y has been taught to work with others and develop a team mindset.

Works Well with Authority

The mentorship relationship between Generation Y and the Baby Boomer Generation is better compared to the one that exists between Generation X and the Baby Boomer Generation. One reason for the positive relationship between Generation Y and the Baby Boomer Generation is that Generation Y tends to work well with authority and those two generations are not in direct competition with each other. However, the relationships between Generation Y and X employees tend to be strained due to competition for the same jobs and career opportunities.

Positive feedback has always been an effective motivational technique with every generation, even more so with this generation. Many in Generation Y were raised by parents who continuously praised them and provided positive feedback for their achievements. Therefore, Generation Y is going to expect similar feedback from their supervisors if positive results are going to be achieved.

Generation Y represents the future generation of employees. Because Generation Y is one of the largest, most educated and civic minded generations in U.S. history, their future influence on the workplace cannot be overstated.

MULTIPLE CAREERS IN ONE LIFETIME

"If only I had chosen a different career or taken a different career path," are the words frequently spoken by someone who has reservations about his/her current job or career choice. Those words reflect the belief that life is short and we have only one opportunity at a career. However, this belief is not as true today as it once was. Sometimes opportunity can knock more than once. When it comes to careers, several factors have created the prospects for a second and sometimes third career opportunity.

If we feel we either picked the wrong career or would like to make a career change, it's not too late to do so, regardless of our age or life situation. Today, we have more career options than ever before and these options are not mutually exclusive. In fact, career options are virtually unlimited. The fundamental economic concept of "opportunity cost" may not be as prevalent when it comes to careers. Opportunity cost refers to the fact that life is filled with choices such that if we decide to do one thing we forego the chance to do something else. With careers, we have the opportunity to experience several careers in our lifetime. In other words, we don't have to necessarily sacrifice one career in order to have another one.

Today, it has become easier and more common for people to experience several careers over their lifetime due to the following factors:

- An increased life expectancy. A longer life expectancy will allow people time to do more things, including the opportunity to experience several careers. People will have more choices about when and where they will work. For example, some people may retire at a later age, others may retire temporarily and later reenter the workforce with a different career, and still others may choose to work on a part-time or intermitted basis.

- Expanded career opportunities resulting from the global economy. The demand for skilled employees is going to increase as globalization continues, creating more opportunities for people to move from one career to another. Globalization will create endless career opportunities for employees with the right skills and the willingness to learn new things.
- Enhanced education and training opportunities. Employees with up-to-date and multiple skills are qualified for more jobs and careers, thus allowing them to more easily move from one career to another. Also, as the global demand for goods and services changes so will the demand for new skills and careers.
- Technological change. Due to the rapid pace of technological innovations, the life expectancies of careers is declining, thus requiring employees to change careers more often. Technological innovations will continue to influence the workplace and the types of careers available.

It was once believed that there was only one path to a given career and if we didn't strictly follow it, our career goal could not be achieved. For most employees, the typical career path would lead to a predictable progression, consisting of promotion within the same department of a given company or finding a similar job with another company in the same industry. The traditional career path would yield a single career.

Today, there is no one path for any given career instead, there are multiple paths available. Everyday, people are crossing over into other careers, sometimes without the traditional degrees or experience required for those careers. Instead of the traditional career path that most of us are familiar with, future career paths are going to be analogous or resemble a "jungle gym." In other words, we may experience a period of lateral transfers, followed by a period of unemployment, followed by a re-entrance into the workforce at either a lower or higher level than our previous position.

We should not view our working life as simply being made up of one career. Instead, we need to think of it as a long term career process which is made up of several careers. At the same time, each career can be used as a stepping stone and learning experience for our future careers. For example, a person may have one career for a given number of years and then move on to another career. Some individuals may experience two careers at once, one as a full-time position and the other as a part-time one, while others may be able to enjoy two part-time careers, simultaneously. There is no longer any reason for not working in the career or careers of our choice.

During the twenty-two years that I have worked at Purdue University Calumet, I've witnessed many examples of people changing careers: from steelworkers becoming teachers, nurses becoming school counselors, lawyers becoming college professors, and teachers becoming engineers, to police officers becoming computer technicians.

Jobs and careers require more skills and experience than in the past. Consequently, people may be able to combine and utilize their total backgrounds to become multi-skilled employees which in turn can help to prepare them for the next paradigm shift.

Today, if we find ourselves at a cross-road in career choices and wondering which career to choose, we can now choose both. Then, we only have to decide which career to pursue first, while simultaneously preparing for a future career. When it comes to career choices, sometimes it is possible to impede the concept of opportunity cost. Only a lack of imagination and an unwillingness to pursue our goals can limit our career options.

CONTINUOUS EDUCATION IS JOB SECURITY

Employment in today's workforce is filled with change and uncertainty. Due to technological changes, the information content of all jobs is rapidly increasing. As a result, skills are becoming obsolete at a faster rate and the life span of all careers is declining. Many companies have gone out of business or are downsizing due to technological innovation and global competition. As a result, most workers are employed without any promise from employers of job security or continual employment. Also, over 65 percent of the U.S. workforce is considered to be "at will" employees, which means they can be terminated without notice, at any time, for any reason and without due process.

In the past, employees could rely on employers, unions, or the government for help in securing employment. However, with "at will" employment on the rise, union membership on the decline, and the government unwilling or unable to help, the primary responsibility for long term employment is on each individual. Gone are the days when a person could expect to work for a single employer or rely on a given career for his/her entire working life. Consequently, many employees are faced with the situation where they can experience, without advance notice, recurring periods of temporary unemployment.

An additional concern for employees is the fact that the type of unemployment that is being experienced at an increasing rate is one that is difficult to remedy, "structural unemployment." Structural unemployment results from skill obsolescence, where jobs or careers have been taken over by new technology, such as computers or robots. Structural unemployment is often considered to be a type of permanent unemployment because once it occurs, the only effective remedy is through reeducation or retraining, which can be expensive and time consuming. Without reeducation, the structurally unemployed person will only be qualified to perform minimum wage jobs. Also, who has the money or the time for reeducation? Consequently, for many structurally unemployed people, there are relatively few employment choices available.

However there is a different type of job security and opportunity for continual employment that is available to those employees willing to earn it. Today, continuous employment and job security are synonymous with continuous education and career development. Consequently, by being proactive, employees can avoid skill obsolescence and structural unemployment through continuous education and training. Employees need to develop their skills with career-related education, training and experience in order to realize continuous employment and career security.

Relatively speaking, the opportunities for continual employment for women, minorities and other disadvantaged groups are more difficult when considering the effects of prejudice and discrimination. Consequently, continuous education and training have even greater significance for people of diverse groups.

Although continuous education can be expensive and time consuming, it is better than experiencing long periods of unemployment and spending even more time and money on reeducating or retraining if suddenly we find ourselves without a job due to obsolete skills. Also, when engaging in continuous education while we are working, we may be fortunate enough to have our employers pay for our education. In either case, education is a direct investment in oneself, with lifetime dividends. Another benefit of education is that it is mobile and can be taken with us to other employment opportunities.

Because of the uncertainty associated with today's economy, employees need skills that are transferable into other jobs, industries and careers. Also employees need to develop multiple skills in case any given skill suddenly becomes obsolete. Having multiple skills that are up-to-date can increase the probability of continuous employment. Employees need to take advantage of any career related training or experience available, including: lateral transfers within their company that can broadening their skills and experience, company sponsored training programs, especially cross-training opportunities, volunteer work, professional affiliations and networking, part-time employment, and attending classes.

Because of technological change, competition from the global economy, longer life spans, and increased educational opportunities, people should expect to change jobs and even careers several times throughout their working lives.

Some of these job and career changes may be voluntarily undertaken while other changes may not. Whether we like it or not, change is going to occur and has become a permanent part of our personal and working life. Therefore, it's important for everyone to be proactive and prepared when change occurs. For those of us who anticipate and are prepared for change, the options available for responding to that change are going to be greater than for those of us who are unprepared for change. Being proactive gives us more alternatives to choose from, while being reactive limits the alternatives available.

Lifelong education and training have become the lifelong responsibility of anyone wanting lifelong employment. In the past, some of us relied on the government, unions or our employers for employment security. However, the days where someone else is going to responsible for our economic well being are long gone and unlikely to ever return. Therefore, to remain marketable and employed, every person must make a commitment to continuous education.

REVIEW QUESTIONS

1. Generation X generally refers to Americans born between what years?
2. How do Generations X and Y feel about company seniority systems?
3. What will the typical career path for most employees in the future look like?
4. Compared with previous generations of workers, Generation X has a desire for jobs that satisfy higher level needs.
5. Generation X has a high regard for authority compared with previous generations of Americans.
6. Younger generations believe that long term employment opportunities can be achieved with a single employer.
7. Generation Y generally refers to Americans born between what years?
8. Why is it easier and more common for a person to experience several careers over his/her lifetime?
9. Continuous education and training are necessary for long term employment.
10. What is the type/category of worker that will increase in the future?

LEARNING ACTIVITIES

1. Divide the class into teams and have each team identify the characteristics of an assigned generation.
2. Have a class discussion on some of the major changes that have occurred in society and how those changes have impacted the workplace.

Issue Nine

Resolving Diversity Related Disputes

"Although we cannot eliminate conflict we can manage it"

Issue Nine deals with a common occurrence that people experience when they interact with one another, conflict. Although some degree of conflict can promote relationship development, too much conflict can have the opposite effect. Because disagreements cannot be avoided, it's important that supervisors develop skills for the effective management of them. By understanding the common causes of conflict, supervisors can establish proactive conflict management strategies.

Managing conflict is even more difficult when diversity is involved. Whenever diverse people interact with each other, there is the increased probability for disagreement and negative results to occur if the conflict is not managed. Because most diversity related disputes in the workplace often involve perceptions of unfairness or discrimination, awareness of the diversity related laws is important. Therefore, any discussion about the management of diversity must include how to effectively resolve conflicts when they occur.

DISAGREEMENT IS A COMMON OCCURRENCE

The changing demographics of the American workforce present supervisors with new challenges when managing diversity. Disagreements among employees with different cultural backgrounds have the potential to disrupt cooperation and teamwork. Resolving conflict can be difficult because of the confusion and misunderstanding about conflict and what to do when it occurs. There are some who feel that conflicts or disagreements should be avoided at all cost in order for a relationship to development. Proponents of this belief feel that all disagreements have negative effects on relationships, especially in the workplace. However, this view about conflict is based on faulty and un-analyzed assumptions about relationship development, teamwork and human behavior.

In reality, disagreements are common occurrences and a natural part of every personal and work relationship. Regardless of how well people like or get along with one another, disagreements will eventually occur. Disagreement is an unavoidable phase of relationship development, but at the same time, when it does happen, should not be ignored. Without some degree of conflict, effective communication and understanding will not take place, and the relationship will not develop.

Most human relations experts believe that disagreements between people are neither good nor bad. What is important when disagreements occur is how they are resolved or managed. At the same time, we should avoid the extremes of either too much or too little conflict. For example, workplace conflicts that occur too often may create unnecessary stress among employees and disruption of the work process, get out of control, and result in small problems escalating into large ones. On the other hand, too little conflict can also present certain problems. For example, without disagreement:

- poor decisions may go unchallenged
- people will tend to be less honest with each other
- problems or new ideas may not be discussed
- unresolved small problems may develop into a major problems
- relationships may not develop
- a negative and extreme type of peer pressure or group conformity may develop, known as "group think"
- indifference or uncaring on the part of the people involved may occur

During the course of every relationship, certain situations may occur which can determine whether a relationship will continue and develop or terminate. A major turning point in every relationship is when a disagreement occurs and how effectively the disagreement is resolved or managed. During the early stages of most relationship, most people try to avoid conflict because they are often uncomfortable and even fearful around each other. Making a positive first impression and try to avoid saying or doing anything that may seem controversial is of paramount importance. Consequently, we are generally less honest with each other and don't behave as we normally would. Examples of other situations where we may want or need to make a positive first impression and therefore, avoid disagreement include:

- interviewing for a new job
- going on a first date
- attempting to sell a product or service to a new customer or client

However, absent the above situations, there is nothing wrong or bad about two people disagreeing with each other. What is important is the effective resolution or management of the disagreement. If the conflict is managed in a positive way, positive change and an improved relationship may result. If the conflict is not managed in an effective way, a break down in communication and the relationship may occur.

When resolving a disagreement, it's important for the parties to separate the issue being discussed, from their relationship. We should not allow a disagreement about a given issue to destroy the relationship. In other words, we should focus on the problem itself and not attack each other personally. However, sometimes that's easier said than done because many disagreements involve emotions responses.

If the disagreement involves some aspect of the relationship, the parties should focus on behaviors and not personalities. Behaviors can be influenced and changed, but not personalities. Also, most relationship problems or disagreements are caused by undesirable behaviors and not personalities. The same can be said for work related problems. For example, if an employee is coming to work late, not performing up to standards or is taking too much time during work breaks, these are behavior problems, not a personality problem. Even if the employee's personality could be changed, the undesirable behavior would persist.

Relationships need to be constantly managed in order for them to grow. When diversity is involved, there is the potential for more conflict to develop due the differences in values, backgrounds and perceptions. At the same time, people need to realize that in every relationship, conflict will eventually occur, but what's most important is how the disagreement is managed. Relationships that have withstood the test of time are those that have experienced conflict and their effective resolution.

RESOLVING DIVERSITY RELATED CONFLICTS

Supervisors face new challenges as the workforce becomes more diverse. Workplace conflicts between employees of different cultures, genders, generations, and backgrounds have become more frequent and can be especially difficult to resolve. Therefore, to be effective leaders, supervisors need to develop conflict management skills that can be used to resolve disagreements between diverse employees.

Every workplace has the potential for conflict, especially those where employees have different values, perceptions and experiences. Additional concerns supervisors encounter when dealing with diverse employees and resolving disagreements is the need to understand the anti-discrimination laws. The perception of unfairness when diversity-related conflicts develop sometimes results in employees filing complaints of employment discrimination. It must be remembered that employees who are considered to be in protected groups represent over 70 percent of the U.S. workforce. At the same time, it doesn't cost employees any money to file complaints of discrimination with federal or state governmental enforcement agencies. Some of the benefits associated with effective conflict resolution:

- avoid lawsuits, especially complaints of employment discrimination
- improve interpersonal relationships, since resolving employee conflicts will often promote greater understanding and cooperation
- solve work-related problems that may be having negative effects on performance and morale

Although disagreements cannot be eliminated, there are guidelines supervisors can follow which can help them to ensure that diversity related ones are effectively managed.

Recognize the Benefits of Conflict

Supervisors must realize that conflict is not necessarily bad. What is important is how it is managed. The ability to maintain a long term relationship is not due to the absence of conflict, but the ability to effectively management it. Without disagreement, we have a tendency to become complacent, allowing bad ideas to go unchallenged or not discussing problems.

Recognize the Benefits of Diverse Thinking

Different thinking styles can promote creative thinking and problem-solving in the workplace. Whenever people with different cultures, perceptions, experiences, and backgrounds interact with each other there is the opportunity for learning to occur as they exchange ideas and ways to do things. Consequently, interaction between employees from different cultures often results in new ideas, practices and products, and innovations.

Maintain a Win-Win Attitude

Many view conflict with the belief that there has to be a winner and loser. However, if we approach a situation with that mindset, it makes effective resolution even more difficult. Instead, we should view conflict with a win-win mindset. Believing there are solutions that can satisfy the needs of both parties will facilitate the resolution process and promote cooperation.

Share Information on the Problem

There should to be an open dialogue between the parties. Often the facts surrounding a disagreement are a combination of objective and subjective information, or a blend of facts and emotions. Conflict resolution is a problem-solving process which requires that relevant information be exchanged.

Define the Problem

Without establishing blame, the problem should be defined from the viewpoints of both parties. Determine what each party wants or what their goals are. It is especially important that we attempt to understand the issues, ideas and feelings of each party when dealing with employees who have different values and worldviews. Sometimes conflict has more to do with insensitivity or ignorance of different cultural values, than with specific work issues. An awareness of the existence of different cultural values can promote understanding and facilitate the resolution process.

Create Cultural Synergy

By combining the perspectives of both parties and identifying a common goal or solution, supervisors can help the parties recognize the benefits of working together. Cooperation and working together can create a positive outcome known as "synergy." Cultural synergy occurs when the goal of each party is merged into one shared goal resulting in mutual satisfaction. By focusing on their similarities and not their differences, ideas can be brainstormed and a common goal or solution identified which can resolve the disagreement.

Develop and Implement a Plan of Action

All the efforts of conflict management will be lost if no action is taken. Therefore, once the agreed upon goal or solution has been identified, a detailed plan of action should be developed to implement the solution. Once the action plan is implemented, the plan needs to be monitored. Also recognize that as time and circumstances change, some modification in the original action plan may be necessary.

Some people choose to deal with conflict by either ignoring it or trying to avoid it. However, if we think of conflict as a natural part of every relationship and abide by the guidelines for managing conflict, greater communication and understanding can result. Globalization will reward those organizations that have supervisors who have developed effective conflict management skills.

DOCUMENT THE RESOLUTION PROCESS

The resolution of disputes between employees or between employees and supervisors can be a time consuming and expensive process, especially if those disagreements are not resolved properly. Workplace conflicts have always created the potential for lawsuits, especially when those disputes involve issues directed related to the welfare of the employees, such as promotion, pay, corrective action, termination or the perception of unfair treatment. What can make the conflict resolution process even more difficult is when the disputes involve employees who have a legally protected status, such women, members of minority groups, employees with disabilities, or employees age 40 years or older. Supervisors should always exercise care when mediating disagreements. However, extra care should be taken when resolving conflicts involving employees belonging to protected groups because of the availability of government agencies for filing complaints and the courts for initiating lawsuits of discrimination.

Many disputes involving people who belong to protected groups can result in complaints of discrimination if there is the perception that unfair treatment has occurred during the employment relationship or the resolution process, or if an unfair result has occurred from the resolution process. Also, while mediating disagreements, emotions and subjectivity can also make the resolution process more difficult.

Today's educated employees are aware of the laws prohibiting employment discrimination and will not hesitate to file complaints with the Equal Employment Opportunity Commission or similar governmental agencies, especially since employees bear no financial cost when filing such complaints. In fact, filing a complaint is so easy that it can be done in person, over the telephone, by mail or email. However, for employers, complaints of discrimination can involve time, money and negative publicity. Also, management will have to deal with the negative rumors resulting from complaints and the effect those rumors can have on morale and performance.

An important and sometimes overlooked part of the resolution process, from the standpoint of liability, is documentation. The old saying, "put it in writing," should be applied to every employment decision made, action taken or procedure followed, including the conflict resolution process. Proper documentation can benefit management by providing evidence of fair and nondiscriminatory treatment. Unfortunately, some supervisors don't document, believing it takes too much time and is unnecessary. Other supervisors only begin to document when they believe a complaint or lawsuit is about to occur. By then, the documentation efforts are of little or no value for the employer. However, it's important for supervisors to document the entire resolution process, in case the parties involved decide to take the dispute outside the company by filing complaints with government enforcement agencies or lawsuit in the courts.

Sometimes employers lose these complaints and lawsuits, not because of any wrongdoing, but because they lack evidence substantiating proper behavior. Some employers and supervisors believe that an employee alleging discrimination must prove the allegation. Although that is true in a court of law, when it comes to governmental enforcement agencies, often the initial burden is placed on the employer or supervisor to justify any action or decision and prove non-discrimination. Consequently, it is one thing to allege innocence or proper behavior and it's another thing to be able to prove it. Therefore, it's important for organizations to provide training on the importance of documentation and how to document.

Documentation can benefit employers and supervisors during the resolution process in several ways:

1. Documentation can discourage employee complaints and lawsuits by providing evidence of equal treatment during the employment relationship and resolution process.
2. Documentation can help employers win lawsuits if they do occur by providing evidence of nondiscriminatory treatment during the employment relationship and resolution process.
3. Documentation can provide management with the opportunity to monitor, evaluate and improve future procedures, behavior and decision-making by establishing a record for later review.

What is meant by documentation? Generally, anything handwritten, printed, recorded or the use of other tangible evidence which can help prove what is being alleged. Most documentation doesn't have to be witnessed or written in a certain format in order for it to be admissible in court. Generally, documentation can be any tangible evidence substantiating an event, procedure, action or decision, including:

1. Personal notes taken during the dispute resolution process.
2. Company policies, procedures and handbooks.

3. Personal notes taken prior to an employment decision.
4. Disciplinary reports and recorded patterns of behaviors.
5. Performance appraisals, attendance records and time sheets.

The more objective and detailed the documentation about the employee's behavior or performance and resolution process, the better the evidence. It is a good business practice to make documentation a regular part of every employment decision, action or procedure. If employers and supervisors document on a regular basis it will eventually become a habit that can pay major dividends in the future.

REVIEW QUESTIONS

1. When a person enters into conflict resolution, he/she should have a "win-lose" attitude.
2. What is meant by "cultural synergy?"
3. Long term harmony in a relationship is the absence of conflict.
4. Parties involved in conflict resolution should share information about the problem.
5. What are two benefits of conflict?
6. Organizations should discourage diverse thinking among employees.
7. What are two benefits of effective conflict resolution?
8. Why should supervisors be aware of the anti-discrimination laws when dealing with conflict?
9. Once an action plan for resolving conflict is developed, the parties should not attempt any modification of that plan.
10. When defining "the problem" during the conflict resolution process, it's important for one of the parties to admit fault.

LEARNING ACTIVITIES

1. Have a class discussion to identify the additional concerns involved when resolving diversity related disputes.
2. Have a class discussion where students speak about some of the conflicts they have had with diverse co-workers and how those conflicts were resolved.

Multicultural Leadership and Teambuilding

"Changing workforce demographics require a new leadership style"

Issue Ten focuses on the importance of developing multicultural leadership and teambuilding skills. Globalization has increased the degree of interaction between nations and diverse people forcing employers and supervisors to have to deal with diversity issues, including the management of a diverse workforce. Over the last several decades, there have been significant changes in the demographics of the American workforce which will require leaders to develop skills that will enable them to effectively manage diversity.

Therefore, success for American businesses is contingent on the abilities of supervisors and employees to understand and work with people of diverse backgrounds and cultures on an organizational, national and international level. Also, because supervisors must make employment decisions on a daily basis and are primarily responsible for the behavior and performance of employees, they must learn how to effectively manage a diverse workforce.

TODAY'S WORKPLACE
REQUIRES MULTICULTURAL LEADERSHIP

Often, the success of an organization depends on the quality of leadership, the role typically performed by supervisors. In most organizations, supervisors are the decision-makers, problem-solvers, and people directly responsible for the behavior and performance of employees. As role models, supervisors can have a major influence on employee attitudes and other work-related concerns. Also, the supervisor's job is multidimensional and can rapidly change with the demands of the work situation. A current challenge confronting the typical supervisor is the need to develop multicultural leadership skills for the following reasons:

1. Gone are the days when American companies primarily competed on a local or national level. Instead, American companies are competing in an international economy which will require that business decisions have long term and global perspectives. Having leaders who understand diverse people and the cultural values of other nations will give American companies a competitive advantage as they continue to provide goods and services throughout the world.
2. Because a supervisor's job will involve interaction with employees from different cultures, the success of a company depends on the effective management of its diverse workforce. The benefits of a properly managed workforce include high performance and job satisfaction, low turnover and absenteeism, and fewer disciplinary problems. Therefore, leaders must develop multicultural leadership skills to be successful.

Guidelines for developing multicultural leadership skills

Understand Different Cultural Values

Workforce diversity will continue into the future as employees with various cultural backgrounds enter the American labor force. Because an employee's thinking and behavior are influenced by culture, effective leadership requires that supervisors have the ability to manage employees with different cultural values. Consequently, supervisors can better communicate and motivate their employees if they have an understanding of their values.

Recognize the Benefits of Diverse Thinking

Effective leaders understand the benefits that can result when diverse employees are involved in decision making and problem solving. Because diverse thinking promotes creative thinking and innovation, interaction between employees from different cultures often leads to new ideas, improved business practices, and better products and services.

Treat Employees as Individuals

The leadership approach of treating every employee the same is outdated and ineffective. Today, it's important for supervisors to treat each employee as an individual and avoid stereotyping based on race, age, gender or other group characteristics. The rule for effective interpersonal relationships in the new millennium focuses on treating employees as individuals by taking the time to learn how each person wants to be treated.

Become a Multidisciplinary Leader

Effective leadership requires broad based knowledge of many disciplines. For example, leaders need to understand different cultural values, technological innovations, safety management and global economics in order to help the organization achieve its goals.

Provide Employee Training

Leaders need to provide training which will enable employees to develop their job related skills and competencies. Additionally, career development, such as mentoring and long term career planning, is an important part of employee training. Career development can promote retention initiatives by helping employees to make the best career choices and improve their opportunities for advancement.

Become a Diversity Role Model

Often, employees will be influenced by the attitudes and behaviors of leaders. Therefore, supervisors need to be positive role models by promoting the benefits of diversity, and promptly addressing prejudicial attitudes and discrimination.

Use Objective and Job Related Evaluation Criteria

Employees should be treated as individuals and evaluated accordingly. Therefore, leaders should use objective and job related criteria when evaluating an employee's performance. Job related criteria will help ensure accurate evaluations and limit complaints of discrimination.

Be Aware of the Anti-Discrimination Laws

When dealing with diversity, it's important for leaders to understand their legal duties and responsibilities in order to avoid behaviors that may violate the anti-discrimination laws. Having a general understanding of Title VII, the Americans With Disabilities Act, and the Age Discrimination in Employment Act can help to limit and address discrimination complaints.

Act As a Team Leader

Cooperation and teamwork are essential for organizational success. Because an organization consists of various teams and work groups, leaders need to develop teambuilding skills.

Effectiveness in today's dynamic economy will require leaders to develop the skills that are conducive for managing in the new business reality. Globalization and workforce diversity are not going to go away and therefore, will require leaders to develop multicultural leadership skills.

"DIFFERENT" EMPLOYEES REQUIRE NEW LEADERSHIP

Globalization and the increased diversity of the American labor force have created the need for a different type of leadership. Traditional leadership styles are not going to be effective with diversity. For organizational success, supervisors must develop new leadership skills that are conducive to managing a diverse workforce.

Understanding people from different cultures, generations and others we perceive to be "different" can help supervisors to effectively interact and manage them. Unfortunately, applying traditional American human relations theories and leadership techniques may not be effective with today's diverse workforce, especially since they have different values, perceptions and world views. These differences can complicate the leadership process because they will force supervisors to constantly update their skills in order to be successful. This can be especially difficult for more experienced supervisors who were successful in the past using tested leadership tactics, but must now learn new leadership skills for future success. The leadership paradigm has shifted once again and skills that made some supervisors successful in the old paradigm may interfere with success in the new paradigm.

Contrasting some of the major characteristics of today's employees with those of traditional employees can help supervisors to better understand the current workforce and promote effective leadership. Table 10.1 contrasts characteristics of traditional employees with those of today's employees.

Ideal Employee

Traditionally, organizations attempted to promote workforce harmony through assimilation, where employees were encouraged to conform to a stereotype of how the ideal employee should look and behave. It was thought that eliminating differences between employees, by attempting to force everyone to be the same, would promote teamwork and organizational effi-

Table 10.1. Contrasting characteristics of traditional with today's employees

Characteristic:	Traditional Employee	Today's Employee
Ideal employee:	assimilated	diversity
Needs:	lower level needs	higher level needs
Career:	one career	multiple careers
Job security:	rely on employer	self reliant
Education:	education helpful	education essential
Work:	work alone	work in teams
Skills:	specialist	multi-skilled

ciency. Today, most diversity experts agree that trying to pressure employees to conform to some subjective and non-job related stereotype is not an effective way to develop relationships or supervise employees. Instead, allowing employees to be different in how they think and get the job done can have major benefits for the organization.

Employee Needs

Traditionally, employees were most concerned with having jobs that satisfied their lower level needs, such as adequate pay, company benefits and safe working conditions. For the most part, satisfying lower level needs was relatively easy for employers to do since money or economic factors were generally the means to do so.

Today, organizations must satisfy other human needs in order to motivate employees. In the new millennium, employees are going to be attracted to those organizations that provide jobs that will satisfy both their lower and higher level needs. Higher level needs refer to psychological needs that can be satisfied by providing jobs that are interesting, challenging and allow the employees to be involved in decision-making and problem solving. Satisfying higher level needs is more difficult because, not only do individual differences have to be taken into consideration but, the needs of each individual employee change overtime.

Career

Traditionally, the career choices for most employees were limited to one career over the course of the employee's working life. As a result, once a given career was chosen, the employee remained in that career until retirement. Today, globalization and technological change has decreased the life span of most careers, thus creating the need to develop new careers.

From now on, employees will have the opportunity to experience several careers throughout their working lives. However, to remain marketable and have the flexibility to leave one career and enter another one, employees will need to develop skills that are transferable into other jobs and careers.

Job Security

Traditionally, employees relied on their employer to provide them with long term employment and job security. Therefore, it was common for most employees to remain with one employer throughout their working lives. Today, with the global economy and rapid technological change, there are no guarantees of job security with a given employer. Instead, long term employment will require that each employee assume the responsibility of ensuring that his/her skills are up-to-date and marketable through continuous education, training and skill development.

Role of Education

In the past, having some amount of post high school education was helpful in pursuing employment opportunities. Today, given the degree of competition for jobs and the need for up-to-date skills, education is essential for a career and advancement. Those employees with limited education are going to experience limited employment opportunities. Also, the primary responsibility for skill updating and education lies with the individual employee.

Nature of Work

In the past, work in most organizations was done independently or in isolation, where employees would work alone and were encouraged to become artisans and craftsmen. Today, most organizations rely on teamwork to complete jobs and achieve organizational goals. The synergistic benefits of teamwork cannot be overstated as American companies attempt to improve their efficiency to satisfy the global demand for goods and services. Therefore it's important for supervisors and employees to understand the components of teambuilding.

Skills

In the past, employees were encouraged to become specialist or develop expertise in a particular job or one aspect of a job. Today, the information and skill content of all jobs is rising which has created the need for multi-skilled employees. Consequently, employees with diverse skills are the type most organizations are hiring and promoting. Because of the changing nature of jobs, becoming multi-skilled gives both the employer and employee more advantages than when an employee has only one skill.

As is true with most skills, effective leadership is a dynamic process requiring continual updating for success. Change is creating new challenges for supervisors, especially in the area of leadership development. Those supervisors who are willing to develop new skills and exercise flexible leadership are going to be successful in the new workforce paradigm.

MULTICULTURAL TEAMBUILDING

Today, most organizations are using the team approach to realize the benefits of synergy and improve overall organizational performance. According to the concept of synergy, the whole is greater than the sum of its parts. In other words, greater output can be achieved by combining resources and working together than by working or using those resources independently. Many organizations have begun to recognize the importance of the whole or team concept for achieving organizational success, especially in light of global competition. As a result, more organizations are providing training for their supervisors on how to develop teams and become effective team leader. Other reasons why team training has become so popular are:

- most work in organizations is done in teams
- employees learn faster and remember information longer with team training
- promotes greater understanding and cooperation between the various departments

Because the U.S. workforce continues to undergo dramatic changes in its size and composition, there is also the need for supervisors to develop the skills necessary to effectively manage multicultural teams. Changing demographics have placed greater emphasis on diversity and multicultural teams. Therefore, to develop comprehensive team skills, supervisors need to understand the components of multicultural teambuilding.

Components of Multicultural Teambuilding

Acknowledge Differences

One false assumption about how to develop multicultural teams is that there should be no mention of the fact that team members are different from one another in terms of culture, race, ethnicity and other factors that distinguishes one person from another. This misperception is based on the belief that differences are divisive factors and acknowledging them may create dissension and interfere in the teambuilding process.

In fact, the key benefits resulting from multicultural teams are due to the differences that exist among team members. A team composed of diversity provides the opportunity to use different thinking styles and alternative approaches to solve problems and get things done. Therefore the leader should acknowledge the diversity that exists among team members and the opportunities diversity presents. Team members must recognize the advantages that a diverse team can offer in solving problems and making decisions, as opposed to a team made up of members who are similar in culture, background and experience.

Focus on Common Goals

While capitalizing on the benefits of diversity, the leader should make similarities that exist among team members the string that holds the team together and build upon those similarities. Similarities that must be emphasized include organizational goals which can only be achieved through cooperation and working together. A way to analogize or think about an organization is that it is a large team made up of smaller teams. Consequently, every employee, supervisor and department must work together if the organization is going to be successful. Working together to achieve common goals will make the organization more productive and benefit everyone.

Identify Skills and Abilities

Before establishing team goals, the leader should evaluate the skills and abilities of every team member. This evaluation of individual members should be undertaken to identify the strengths and weaknesses of each member, what role each member can perform in the team, and what members can do to improve their skills.

Establish Goals and Timetables

Establishing short term and long term goals will help to give the team a sense of purpose and direction. At the same time, team goals and timetables must be realistic, challenging and measurable. The abilities, skills and experiences of team members will influence what the team can accomplish and the timetables for achieving those goals. For example, a team made up of highly motivated, experienced and competent members should be expected to accomplish more and in a shorter time than a team made up of less motivated, experienced and competent members.

Define the Role of the Team Leader

To create understanding and avoid disappointment, the leader should identify his/her role as the team leader. This will create understanding, not only for the members but also the leader. How the team and its members are going to be evaluated, what team members can expect from the leader in terms of support, and what type of leadership style will be used, are some examples of how the leader might define his/her roles.

Define the Roles of Team Members

It's important for the leader and each member to discuss the responsibilities of each team member. This will help each member to better understand and accept his/her roles. Members must understand the interdependent nature of a team and that team success is dependent on how well members cooperate and work together to achieve common team goals.

Establish Mutual Support

During the early stages of team development, members tend to act as individuals and out of self-interest. The leader and members need to understand that it takes time for the team to become self-directed and for members to develop trust and mutual respect for each other. At the same time, members must learn to support and provide constructive feedback to each other in order for the team to develop a productive working relationship.

Manage Conflict

Conflict or disagreement between employees cannot be eliminated. Because interpersonal conflict is an inevitable part of any working relationship, developing conflict management skills are essential for team leadership. The potential for conflict is greater when teams are composed of members with diverse cultures, backgrounds and life experiences. Leaders and employees must understand that conflict is a part of every workplace, but what's most important is the effective management of that conflict.

Evaluate Team Performance

Team effectiveness is determined by team results and progress. Objective and job related performance criteria should be used to ensure accurate evaluations. The leader needs to evaluate the strengths and weaknesses of the team and individual members on a regular basis, and provide timely and specific feedback.

Continuous Monitoring

Long-term team success requires the leader to be proactive in order to anticipate and prepare for changing circumstances. The leader and team members must avoid becoming complacent and should continue to monitor team progress and implement change when and where it is needed.

The benefits associated with teams are going to make teambuilding an important component of managerial development. At the same time, workforce diversity has placed emphasis on multicultural teambuilding.

REVIEW QUESTIONS

1. Supervisors should be diversity role models.
2. Why is teambuilding important?
3. When developing multicultural teams, leaders should define their role(s).
4. Teams should avoid discussing diversity-related issues.
5. A team should develop long-term team goals.
6. Supervisors should evaluate employees using objective and job related criteria.
7. What is an example of career development training?
8. Why do supervisors need to become multicultural leaders?
9. What is a benefit of effective teamwork?
10. What is an example of negative synergy?

LEARNING ACTIVITIES

w2. Have a class discussion where students talk about their experiences with effective and ineffective leaders.

Sexual Orientation and the Workplace

"Information provides the opportunity for understanding"

Issue Eleven deals with the controversial and misunderstood issue of sexual orientation. Understanding the concerns of gay and lesbian employees represents an often overlooked and yet, important diversity issue. As is true with every diverse group, there is more commonality that exists between groups than differences. Also, globalization has highlighted the importance of utilizing and effectively managing the talents of all employees, regardless of their sexual orientation.

Although there is no federal law prohibiting employment discrimination against gay and lesbian employees in the private employment sector, there are state, county and municipal laws that supervisors and employees need to be aware of. Also, it's important for supervisors to understand how to effectively interact with gay employees, not only because they represent a vital component of diversity, but because of the impact they can have on organizational teamwork and performance.

PREVENTING DISCRIMINATION AGAINST GAY AND LESBIAN EMPLOYEES

Gay and lesbian employees represent a significant, but often overlooked component of organizational diversity. Recognizing the shortage of skilled labor, the competition for qualified employees, and the unlimited global demand for goods and services, organizations cannot afford to disregard or underutilize any source of human capital. Unfortunately, gay and lesbian employees are often victims of negative stereotyping, prejudice and discrimination. Any group

105

of employees who feel unappreciated and discriminated against will not re-main with an organization for any length of time. Therefore, employers and su-pervisors need to be future oriented and develop strategies to prevent or limit negative stereotyping and unfair treatment based on sexual orientation.

Strategies to Prevent sexual Orientation Discrimination

Company Policy

Many organizations have implemented policies and practices prohibiting dis-crimination based on sexual orientation. These companies recognize that such policies are necessary for organizational success and are in the best interest of all employees. In some organizations these policies are a part of the com-pany's overall harassment and discrimination policies. Such policies are an indication to supervisors and employees that the organization is concerned about their welfare and serious about protecting the rights of everyone. Not only will these policies prevent unfair treatment, they will also limit com-plaints and lawsuits of discrimination.

Laws

Everyday, society's changing attitudes are being reinforced by new laws and court decisions. As social attitudes toward gay and lesbian people become more tolerant and accepting, laws governing society and the workplace will reflect these new beliefs. Although there is no federal law prohibiting dis-crimination based on sexual orientation in the private employment sector, there are state, county and municipal laws, and court decisions which prohibit such discrimination. Also, it's only a matter of time before a federal law pro-hibiting discrimination based on sexual orientation is enacted. Changing atti-tudes and laws require organizations to be proactive and anticipate future trends.

Education and Training

As is true with most concerns, being informed is essential for eliminating or reducing negative stereotypes, prejudice and discrimination associated with gay and lesbian employees. Providing awareness training and educa-tion programs are effective ways for employers to raise the issue and pro-mote the understanding of lifestyle diversity. Employees must be made aware that just as there is diversity about the way people look, think, and behave, so there is diversity in lifestyles and sexual orientations. Relevant information can help employers, supervisors and employees resist the negative myths, fears and stereotypes about gay employees. In addition to providing training about the laws and company policies dealing with sexual orientation, educational programs should also include discussions on the following issues: (1) religious beliefs, (2) sexual activity, (3) personal choice, and (4) fear of "differences."

(1) Religious Beliefs

Some people believe that a gay lifestyle conflicts with morality or religion. They feel that tolerance or acceptance of the lifestyle of gay and lesbian employees would be a violation of their moral or religious beliefs. However, fairness requires that everyone have equal rights which should include the right to have different beliefs about lifestyles and morality. As long as one's rights do not interfere with or subjugate those of another, a person's lifestyle should be a personal matter and a protected right. Also, from the standpoint of fairness, supervisors should evaluate all employees, including gay employees, on objective and job related criteria, not their lifestyle or sexual orientation.

When considering religion, managing diversity requires at a minimum, that we tolerate differences that exist among people. While some religious beliefs may make it difficult to accept a gay sexual orientation, it should be remembered that other religions are tolerant or accepting of it. Therefore, managing diversity requires tolerance for different people, along with their lifestyles, even if we don't agree with them.

(2) Sexual Activity

Unfortunately, some people believe that the principal concern of gay and lesbian employees is about sex or sexual activity. According to this belief, gay people are promiscuous and only interested in having sex. As is true with most stereotypes, this belief of gay people is unfair and not true.

In fact, many of the concerns confronting gay employees are similar to those of heterosexual employees. At the same time, overcoming stereotypes about different people sometimes begins with the use of terminology that can help avoid confusion or misunderstanding. As a result, using politically acceptable terms when referring to people associated with different groups can promote understanding. For example, to deemphasize the notion of sex, the term "transgender" has replaced the term "transsexual."

(3) Personal Choice

Some people believe that being gay is a preference or personal choice, and therefore, a gay person can change his/her sexual orientation. Additionally, some people believe that if they associate with gay people, they might convert their sex orientation and also become gay. However, most diversity research concludes that people are born with a given sexual orientation that does not change or cannot be changed. Consequently, the politically correct term is "sexual orientation," not "sexual preference."

However, even if a gay lifestyle was a choice, the right to choose one's lifestyle is a right organizations should not attempt to interfere with or infringe upon. At the same time, if there was a choice on being gay, this choice would not be a legitimate management concern because it doesn't affect employee performance or any other job related interest. Managing diversity includes the right to be "different."

(4) Fear of "differences"

Fear of people we perceive to be "different" can sometimes cause us to react emotionally instead of objectively. A major source of fear is the lack of information about something, in other words, fear of the unknown. A lack of information tends to create rumors, misperceptions, and stereotypes about gay people. For those people who do not understand gay issues or their lifestyle, there is a tendency to be fearful and to react with prejudice and discriminatory behavior. Fear resulting from misunderstanding can also cause us to avoid associating with gay people, which can lead to further alienation and discrimination. However, learning more about gay people as individuals can promote understanding and reduce negative myths, fears, and stereotypes about them.

Managing diversity requires every organization to be proactive in dealing with the concerns of employees. Many of the issues confronting gay and lesbian employees are the same issues heterosexual employees are concerned about. At the same time there are issues that are particularly relevant for gay and lesbian employees that organizations need to address in order to prevent discrimination.

COMPANIES MUST DEAL WITH SEXUAL ORIENTATION ISSUES

Employers and supervisors are confronted with new challenges as the labor force becomes more diverse. Although gay and lesbian employees represent approximately 10 percent of the U.S. labor force, until recently, they were considered to be the invisible employees in most organizations. Because of the misperceptions about gay people and the fear of prejudicial and discriminatory actions toward them, many gay employees prefer to keep their sexual orientation a secret. As a result, in many organizations the concerns confronting gay and lesbian employees have not been adequately considered or addressed. However, some organizations are beginning to raise the issue, having recognized the importance in valuing and effectively managing gay and lesbian employees. Regardless of how heterosexual employers, supervisors and employees feel about the issue of sexual orientation, organizations need to be proactive in discussing the issue for several reasons.

Laws

Although there is no national law prohibiting discrimination in employment based on sexual orientation in the private employment sector, there are 11 states and over 170 city and county laws prohibiting such discrimination. Also, more judges are recognizing gay rights and issuing decisions prohibiting sexual orientation discrimination in private sector employment. At the federal level, President Clinton, in 1998, issued Executive Order 13087 which protects federal employees from employment discrimination based on sexual orientation. Many civil rights experts expect a federal law prohibiting such discrimination in the private employment sector within the next 5 years. Therefore, employers need to become future oriented by developing company policies prohibiting discrimination based on sexual orientation.

Recruitment and Retention

In every industry, American companies are currently experiencing a critical shortage of qualified employees. This shortage has affected many organizations in their ability to provide goods and services for the growing global economy. Also, global competition has highlighted the need for American companies to maximum the production of goods and services at the lowest price and with highest quality. As a result, employers cannot afford to overlook any productive and talented pool of labor that can help make the organization more efficient and satisfy global demand. Businesses need to realize that they are competing with other companies for the limited supply of skill labor.

Therefore, employers must develop creative strategies to attract and retain all qualified persons, regardless of their sexual orientation. Employers need to develop a work environment that is "diversity friendly," where all employees are accepted for who they are and valued for their individual contributions.

Gay Consumers

Prosperity in today's global economy requires that organizations satisfy the needs of all consumers. No organization is so successful that it can afford to ignore any consumer group. Therefore, the incomes and buying preferences of gay consumers cannot be overlooked. Providing goods and services for the gay community requires an understanding of their spending habits and the ability to effectively interact with them. Therefore, organizations with gay employees will be in a better position to understand and satisfy the consumer needs of the global gay community. Also, the reputation of an organization which is perceived as "diversity friendly" can promote positive goodwill among consumers.

Organizational Performance

For an organization to be successful, the interdependent nature of the organization requires that all employees work together. The level of cooperation among employees affects the overall performance of a company and therefore, its ability to compete. Regardless of how heterosexual employees feel about gay co-workers, they must understand the importance of teamwork and learn to effectively work together. Globalization has left employees in every organization with the choice of either realizing success by working together to achieve common goals or suffer the economic consequences of inefficiency, downsizing and insolvency.

Social Attitudes

Social values and attitudes are often expressed in the workplace. In other words, what's happening in the workplace is often a reflection of what is happening in society. Therefore, supervisors need to be aware of changing social attitudes and events. For example, drug use and violence in society are also problems encountered in the workplace. Likewise, society's increased acceptance of the gay lifestyle means the workplace will be influenced in a similar manner. At the same time, changing attitudes are encouraging gay employees to accept and express their gay sexual orientation. Public opinion will encourage employers and supervisors to behave in nondiscriminatory ways toward gay employees and base employment decisions on objective and job related criteria, not on an employee's sexual orientation.

Globalization and workforce diversity are forcing every organization to review their policies and behavior toward employees, and implement changes where needed. In the new millennium, organizations that do not adequately address the issue of sexual orientation will suffer negative economic consequences, while those organizations that do will experience positive results.

TERMINOLOGY

Interacting with people who we perceive to be different can be uncomfortable and confusing, especially if we have little or no experience, or information about them. As supervisors, it's important to have broad based knowledge about the different groups we are managing. Workforce diversity has placed a premium on those supervisors who have the skills to effectively interact with various groups. One group that is growing in prominence and yet, misunderstood is gay and lesbian employees. Knowing the terminology that is typically associated with certain groups can form the foundation for understanding and relationship development. The following terminology is frequently encountered when discussing issues or concerns related to sexual orientation.

Transgender

"Transgender" is the politically correct term for a person who used to be referred to as "transsexual." A transgender is a person who believes s/he was born in the wrong body. A transgender believes s/he has the mind of one gender and the body of another. They are men who are living as women and vice versa. If they could afford to, many transgender people would opt for sex change operations. Also, to deemphasize the aspect of "sex" and promote understanding, "gender" has replaced "sexual."

Metrosexual

"Metrosexual" is a term that is used to describe heterosexual men who have a preference for the latest fashions in clothing and personal appearance. It refers to men who are comfortable enough with their sexuality to attend grooming spas, and express their feelings and emotions without embarrassment or concern about how others might perceive them. For example, over a decade ago, most heterosexual men wouldn't consider wearing a pink dress shirt, having manicured finger nails, wearing "men's makeup", or styling and coloring their hair because it wasn't considered to be masculine. Just as the line between minority and non-minority is becoming blurred with time, so is the perception of what is considered to be masculine and feminine.

Civil Unions

"Civil Unions" are similar to marriage licenses for gay couples and have been officially recognized in other countries and the states of Vermont and Connecticut. With the exception of the state of Massachusetts, gay couples cannot legally get married in the U.S. Therefore, some states have approved of civil unions which are legally recognized relationships that give gay couples most of the rights, protections and benefits of marriage. However, it is unclear whether Vermont's and Connecticut's civil unions will be recognized by other states or how many other states will establish their own civil unions.

Transvestite

Don't confuse a transgender with a transvestite. Transvestite refers to a person who likes or has a preference to wear (articles of) the clothing of another gender. Transvestites can be either heterosexual or gay. At the same time, we must be aware that the line between what is male and female attire and grooming habits has become faded in recent years.

Defense in Marriage Acts

Over 30 states and the federal government have "Defense in Marriage Acts" which mandate that marriage can only exist between a man and a woman. However, in November of 2003, the Massachusetts's Supreme Court held that the state constitution guarantees gay couples the right to marry. It remains to be seen how many other states will follow Massachusetts and recognize gay marriages (same-sex marriages).

Sexual Orientation

"Sexual orientation" refers to our natural sexual predisposition for a person of a given gender. Most research and diversity experts believe that a person's sexual orientation is not a matter of choice, but is determined at birth. In other words, people are born either heterosexual or homosexual, and their sexual orientation cannot be changed.

Sexual orientation has replaced the term "sexual preference" to avoid misunderstanding and emphasize the fact that a person's orientation is not a choice. Although no federal law prohibits sexual orientation discrimination in the private employment sector, there are state and municipal laws which prohibit such employment discrimination.

Sex Discrimination

"Sex discrimination" is discrimination based on gender. The term "sex" refers to the condition of being male or female, not sexual practices, activities, beliefs, or orientation. Sex discrimination means that a person is being treated unfairly because of that person's gender.

Sexual harassment is a violation of Title VII of the 1964 Civil Rights Act. Examples of illegal sexual harassment include: a male(s) harassing only females because of their gender and vice versa, or a male(s) harassing only other males because of their gender or a female(s) harassing only other females because of their gender (same-sex harassment).

Gay and lesbian employees represent a growing and significant source of skilled labor. More than ever before, supervisors need to develop "diversity friendly" leadership skills. Familiarity with the terminology associated with gay and lesbian employees can help to avoid misunderstanding and promote relationship development.

REVIEW QUESTIONS

1. What is meant by the term, "transgender?"
2. "Same-sex" harassment is illegal under federal law.
3. The majority of U.S. employers have domestic partner benefits programs.
4. What percent of the U.S. workforce is comprised of gay and lesbian employees?
5. What role do social values and attitudes have on the workplace?
6. What is the federal law prohibiting discrimination in employment based on sexual orientation?
7. What is meant by the term "metrosexual?"
8. Why is sexual orientation an important issue in recruitment and retention?
9. Why is sexual orientation an important issue for organizational performance?
10. What are two concerns gay employees encounter in the workplace that heterosexual employees do not?

LEARNING ACTIVITIES

1. Introduce the topic of gay and lesbian employees to the class by asking questions about sexual orientation.
2. Have a class discussion about work related concerns that are specific to gay employees.

Developing a Diversity Program

"Being proactive and responsive to change are required for organizational success"

Issue Twelve focuses on how to implement diversity related changes in the workplace and the importance of developing a diversity program. Employers must avoid becoming complacent and recognize that change is essential for the future success of an organization. Whether an organization is prepared or not, diversity related issues will continue to dominate the workplace. Therefore, it's imperative for organizations to be future oriented and responsive to changing situations.

A diversity program should be part of an organization's strategic planning. This type of program can prevent problems from developing in the first place by helping to establish a "diversity friendly" work environment that will benefit everyone. Also, as change agents, supervisors will play major roles in facilitating the change process.

ORGANIZATIONAL CHANGE IS IMPORTANT
FOR DIVERSITY

The increased diversity of the American workforce, the need to recruit and retain the best qualified employees, and competing in the global economy have forced organizations to play a larger role in helping its human resources to achieve their personal and professional goals. Management has come to realize that by helping employees to achieve their goals, organizational goals can also be achieved. One way to simultaneously promote the goals of management and employees is through the development of an inclusive organizational culture. Consequently, the business community has recognized the benefits that can result from the creation of an inclusive workplace. Through a diversity program, management and the employees can work together to achieve inclusiveness and enhance organizational performance. A diversity program can both improve the welfare of the employees by helping them to satisfy their personal and professional goals and promote organizational goals.

In order to successfully implement a diversity program, management must be aware of and overcome the major barriers or resistance that may be encountered.

Major Barriers to a Diversity Program

Fear of Change

Because of the unknown consequences that may occur with a given change, it's natural for people to initially resist the implementation of any change, including a diversity program. The uncertainty associated with the program and whether its consequences will be positive or negative for the organization often creates initial fear and resistance on the part of the employees. To overcome this type of resistance, management needs to provide timely information and involve everyone in the change process.

Not a Business Concern

Some managers view a diversity program as a luxury or fringe benefit, and not an economic necessity. According to this view, managing diversity is basically an ethical or moral concern and not a legitimate business issue. However, it's important for management and the employees to realize that a diversity program is economically required for the survival and success of the organization.

Appropriate Leadership Style

Not all leadership styles are conducive to a diversity program. Consequently, the leadership style required for the successful implementation of a diversity program is one that allows all supervisors and employees to be informed and involved in the change process. Therefore, most diversity experts consider a participative leadership style to be the most effective for the successful implementation of the program.

Narrow Definition

To overcome resistance to change, everyone must benefit from it. Unfortunately, some supervisors and employees believe that a diversity program is the same as an affirmative action program and will only benefit women and minority groups. Management should emphasize that the term "diversity" includes everyone, and a diversity program is an inclusive program which will benefit all employees, including white males.

Not Needed

There is the belief that a diversity program is not necessary because women and minorities have made enough progress in being hired and promoted. According to this belief, organizations should focus on equal employment opportunity. Unfortunately, even with equal employment opportunity, negative stereotyping, prejudice, and discrimination still exist in many organizations. A diversity program is designed to create an inclusive work environment, where all employees have an opportunity to advance and achieve their potential. Nevertheless, equal employment opportunity is an important part of a diversity program.

Reverse Discrimination

Some view a diversity program as a form of reverse discrimination, where certain groups benefit at the expense of other groups. According to this belief, unqualified or less competent women and minorities will be hired instead of the best qualified people. However, to ensure that the best qualified people are hired and promoted, a diversity program must place emphasis on the use of objective and job related criteria when making employment decisions. Also, in order for such a program to be successful, it must benefit every individual and group in the organization.

Financial Cost

Nothing is completely free, including a diversity program. There are certain costs associated with implementing a diversity program, such as the costs associated with training and education on diversity, organizational assessment costs, and costs incurred to promote diversity recruitment and retention. However, if the program is implemented in an effective manner, any costs incurred will be short term while the benefits resulting from the program will be long term.

In the future, global interactions and workforce diversity will continue to grow and impact how organizations are managed. Through the implementation of diversity programs, organizations can become future oriented by promoting inclusiveness and simultaneously satisfying the various needs of management and the employees. At the same time, these programs can help ensure long term organizational success.

A DIVERSITY PROGRAM IS PROACTIVE MANAGEMENT

A recent development in human resources management is the need for organizations to create an inclusive workplace. The benefits of diversity are well documented along with the importance of effectively managing a diverse workforce. "Managing diversity" is accomplished by making changes in the organizational culture through the implementation of a diversity program. This type of program is not the same thing as an affirmative action program, nor does it only benefit women, minorities and other traditionally disadvantaged groups. A diversity program is a proactive and long term approach for addressing the needs of all employees, including non-minority males. It is designed to create an inclusive work environment where all employees are accepted and valued as individuals, and have the opportunity to develop and achieve their potential, regardless of their differences.

Every organization has unique characteristics that need to be taken into consideration when implementing a new program or making any change. At the same time, diversity programs vary from one organization to another depending on several factors such as the degree of inclusiveness that currently exist in the organization and its diversity goals. However, there are similar components that most diversity programs have in common with each other.

Major Components of a Diversity Program

Diversity or Cultural Assessment

Before implementing any change, it's important for management to examine the status quo or current organizational culture. An assessment of the organization is required to collect and analyze information about its culture, identify problems such as over-concentration or underutilization of diverse employees in certain job categories, and evaluate existing conditions and systems. Some of the organizational systems or processes that should be evaluated include:

* recruitment and hiring processes
* performance appraisal and promotion processes

- discipline, layoff and discharge procedures
- company benefits and services offered
- career development and training opportunities, and
- the compensation system

One of the worse things management can do is to implement changes without understanding the current situation or considering the consequences of those changes. Not only can such changes create unnecessary stress and disruption, but they can also be wasteful and even counterproductive.

As is true when attempting to solve any problem or improve a situation, understanding the current organizational culture is crucial to determining what changes need to be made. Likewise, the cultural assessment will provide information for making decisions and taking the actions needed to create a "diversity friendly" work environment.

Diversity Goals

It's important for organizations to establish short term and long term diversity goals, along with timetables for creating achieving those goals. The diversity goals should be as specific and quantifiable as possible in order for the organization to accurately measure progress. Not only will the goals provide management and the employees with a sense of purpose and direction, but as the company makes progress toward inclusiveness, the changing culture will further reinforce the program. In order for diversity goals to become a reality, they need to be part of the short term and long term business goals of the organization.

Strategic Planning

Strategic planning is about planning for the future. Along with the establishment of diversity goals, there is the need to develop a detailed and long term plan of action for achieving those goals. This action plan should be future-oriented and identify the steps or phases the organization must proceed through as it moves toward inclusiveness. As is true with any long term plan, sometimes modifications need to be made to the plan as circumstances change.

Evaluation Criteria

Before starting a diversity program, criteria to evaluate the progress and success of the program should be established. "What gets measured gets done" is often a fact of life in many organizations. The evaluation criteria should include measurable results, such as;

- an increase in the number of women and minorities hired and promoted
- a reduction in the number of discrimination complaints filed
- an increase in employee services offered
- an increase in positive comments from employee surveys and focus groups, and
- an increase in the number of career development and training programs offered

Program Support

The success of a diversity program depends on a commitment of time, energy and support from everyone within and outside the organization. It's important for management, the employees, and the community to work together and become actively involved in planning and implementing the program. Getting everyone involved, and keeping them informed as to what is happening and expected to happen will help ensure commitment and accepted.

Utilize Existing Systems and Personnel

Before an organization considers making any major changes, it should attempt to utilize existing systems and personnel within the organization. Training can be instrumental in developing current personnel. Modifying existing systems and making use of current personnel are less expensive, threatening and disruptive than rebuilding the organization from scratch.

Training and Educational Opportunities

A major aspect of being proactive is to anticipate future organizational concerns, including training and educational needs. Global competition and new technology will continue to force every organization to become future oriented in order to be prepared to meet new challenges. Consequently, part of any change initiative is the need for continuous training. As the diversity program proceeds, training and educational programs that deal with the specific needs of the organization will be necessary to satisfy current and future diversity concerns. Some examples of training an organization may consider implementing include:

- training to update employee skills
- leadership development programs, including mentoring programs
- training to reinforce of the benefits of diversity
- training on how to deal with prejudice and discrimination

- training on the equal employment opportunity laws
- training on new company policies
- other training initiatives to reflect changing circumstances

Equal Employment Opportunity and Affirmative Action

Although equal employment opportunity and affirmative action have been in existence for over forty years, many of the concerns that led to their development still exist today. Consequently, because many diversity-related concerns, such as harassment and discrimination, and the recruitment, hiring and promotion of women and minorities require immediate action, equal employment opportunity and affirmative action should remain high priorities. Because a diversity program is a continuous endeavor, equal employment opportunity and affirmative action can be used to achieve both short term and long term diversity goals.

Reinforce the Positive Change

As an organization continues to make progress toward achieving an inclusive environment, any improvements should be reinforced with policies, positive feedback, compensation, training and the dissemination of information about those improvements. Reinforcement will encourage further improvements. Anytime a given behavior or change is reinforced, there is an increased probability for that behavior or change to become permanent.

Monitor and Improve

As an organization achieves success toward creating a "diversity friendly" workplace, it must avoid becoming complacent. Sometimes success can blind an organization to the need for continual change and improvement. Because managing diversity is a process and not an end result, it's important for the organization to avoid becoming satisfied with its accomplishments, but instead continue to be proactive in addressing diversity-related issues. Regardless of how successful the diversity program is, there is always room for improvement.

Change is difficult for most organizations to initiate and adjust to. However, globalization and workforce diversity have made certain changes a necessary part of organizational survival. A diversity program will benefit management and the employees, and help ensure organizational success.

ORGANIZATIONS NEED PROACTIVE CHANGE

Change is important for the success of every organization in every industry. If an organization does not change, it won't be able to make improvements or respond to new challenges. Given the degree of uncertainty organizations are confronted with as the globalization process continues, major adjustments are going to be required on the part of every organization.

Unfortunately, some organizations change only when they are forced to, generally in response to problems that require immediate resolutions in order for the organization to continue to function. For example, an organization may experience an increase in harassment and discrimination lawsuits, and as a result, initiate diversity training. Unfortunately, organizations that passively wait for problems to develop before they make changes are simply reacting to problems or situations as they appear. By being reactive, the options available to those organizations are limited and their ultimate response may either be too late to prevent or correct the problem, or may only result in a temporary and unsatisfactory resolution.

Those organizations that continue to be successful are the ones that are proactive. They anticipate potential problems, and are prepared to either prevent those problems from occurring in the first place or have solutions available before problems occur. For example, as an organization becomes more diverse, training should be implemented to discuss relevant diversity issues, such harassment and discrimination. Being proactive gives an organization more options to choose from when problems arise, more time to consider the consequences of any given response, and the opportunity to make careful and informed decisions. Thus, they are able to increase the probability that the best course of action will be chosen and followed.

With any contemplated change, there are factors that favor that change and factors that oppose it. Examples of factors that may favor a given change might include the recognition on the part of management that in order to effective compete, skill development training must be initiated, new technology introduced into the workplace and different marketing strategies must be utilized. Examples of factors that may oppose a given change might include the resistance by employees of having to learning new skills and technology.

Consequently, before taking action or implementing a change, an organization should conduct a "change assessment" to identify those factors that favor and oppose any given change effort. If properly done, this assessment will help reduce the time required for the organization to adjust to the change by ensuring that all potential concerns have been considered and addressed.

An often overlooked aspect of change is the adjustment period organizations must endure in order to adapt to the changed situation. Part of this adjustment period includes the time required for employees to accept the change and learn how to work in the new environment. Generally, organizations will experience an initial decline in overall performance as old behaviors are unlearned and new behaviors learned. This decline in performance is often attributed to what is commonly referred to as the "learning curve," the time period during which new behaviors, skills and operating procedures are learned. However, if the change is successfully implemented, the duration and the magnitude of the decline in organization performance will be limited.

It must be remembered that any given change experienced by an organization will affect everyone and everything in the organization. Therefore, in order for the change to be successfully implemented, everyone needs to be informed and involved in the change process. At the same time, supervisors will play a pivot role with most changes that occur within an organization. Supervisors are the principal "change agents" responsible for introducing and successfully implementing change. However, for a change to be implemented in the shortest time and with the least disruption, the employees also need to be involved in the change process. Keeping the employees informed and allowing them the opportunity to have some input into the decision-making and problem solving process associated with a given change is important for the change to have positive results.

An example of a change that organizations need to be proactive with is the implementation of a diversity program. A diversity program can help an organization achieve the following diversity goals:

- compete in the global economy
- manage a diverse workforce
- create an inclusive work environment

As is true with most changes, there is an adjustment period associated with implementing a diversity program. The amount of time an organization will need to adjust to the execution of a diversity program will vary depending on what the goals of the program are, the organizational culture that existed prior to the program, and the support the program receives from both management and the employees.

Most people prefer the status quo and tend to resist any change initiative. However, organizational change can be a positive experience, and have long term benefits for the organization if the change is properly implemented. By being proactive, an organization can improve its chances for the effective implementation of any given change and increase its prospects for success.

DON'T OVERLOOK DIVERSITY TRAINING

The rapid pace of globalization and technological change has placed American businesses at a crossroads, forcing them to become proactive in order to anticipate and address future organizational concerns affecting their survival and success. The key to long term success for American businesses is to identify and develop strategies that will allow them to maximize their competitiveness and spur economic growth. One challenge that should be part of every organization's strategic planning is the development of relevant training programs.

Training can satisfy a number of concerns the organization, supervisors and employees may have, such as:

* update and develop employee skills
* improve communication and teamwork
* reduce employee complaints and lawsuits
* improve leadership skills, and
* prepare the organization to respond to new challenges

Training programs should be designed to address current or potential concerns of the organization. In other words, training programs need to be customized for each organization. Therefore, before implementing a training program, companies need to decide:

(1) what type of training is required, and
(2) who will provide the training, in-house or outside trainers

Before making any decision, options need to be explored to identify the advantages and disadvantages associated with choosing a given alternative. Therefore, when deciding who will provide the training, organizations should consider the following:

Advantages of using in-house trainers:

* less expense
* flexible scheduling of training sessions
* better understanding of organizational problems
* training that is directly related to solving actual problems confronting the organization

Advantages of using outside trainers:

* new ideas and business practices can be introduced
* easier to provide constructive feedback to management and the employees
* easier to deal with controversial and emotional organizational issues
* greater sense of expertise when outside "experts" are used

Training needs are a continuous concern for organizations. Therefore, organizations must carefully consider the different training programs available that will help them to compete in the global economy. Training to promote an understanding of global market conditions, technological innovations, and safety management are just a few of the training needs organizations have. Another type of training that organizations need to provide is diversity training.

Diversity Training

In response to globalization and workforce diversity, many businesses and governmental entities are implementing diversity training programs. Diversity training is a proactive type of training with interrelated short term and long term training components which are designed to address the training needs associated with a diverse workforce. Different training modules are designed to provide supervisors with the skills necessary for managing a diverse workforce. The training modules can be conducted during a single training session or over the course of several sessions. Diversity training is sometimes provided as an independent component of an organization's comprehensive training program. Although diversity training programs vary among organizations, they all contain certain components

Components of a Diversity Training Program

Employment Laws and Regulations

As social norms and values change, so will the laws and regulations affecting the workplace. Updating supervisors and employees on the equal employment opportunity laws and affirmative action regulations should be done on a regular basis to limit complaints and lawsuits of harassment and discrimination. Training on the company's employment policies and practices should also be incorporated.

Career Development

Career development has both short term and long term training components. As the information content of jobs change, employees will need to not only update the skills for their current jobs, but develop additional skills to meet future challenges. Competency training is designed to help employees update and develop their job related skills. This training should be available to all employees, with particular emphasis placed on women and minority groups to ensure they are not left behind.

Another training aspect that needs to be incorporated involves the development of technological competence. Regardless of the job being performed, technology will impact that job. Future trends in the global economy will continue to focus on technological innovations, and the integration and automation of company operations, along with the virtual workplace.

Finally, mentoring and long term career planning are necessary to help employees make the best career choices and improve their opportunities for successful careers by preparing them for the next paradigm shift. Career development can also be an important component of an employee retention program.

Multidisciplinary Leadership Skills

To improve leadership, skills will need to reflect the future workforce and business environment. Because business is more multifaceted and dynamic, leaders must have the skills and knowledge that will allow them to make quick decisions involving various disciplines. The complexity and challenges of globalization have placed greater significance on the development of multicultural, multigenerational and multidisciplinary leadership skills.

Communication Skills

Successful management requires effective communication skills since virtually everything a leader does involves some form of communication. Often supervisors serve as official or unofficial management spokespersons by communicating information throughout the organization and the community. Also, communication skills are necessary to promote teamwork and facilitate company operations which may be located in different geographic areas.

Teambuilding

Closely related to communication is teambuilding. Teamwork in the new millennium will be more complicated and interrelated than ever before. Managing teams within the company and across geographic boundaries will require leaders to develop comprehensive teambuilding skills.

Also, working in teams will remain important for the employees, as they continue to deal directly with customers, and participate in problem-solving and decision-making. It is essential for management and the employees, work groups, departments, and facilities separated by geographic distances to communicate and work together if the enterprise is going to be successful.

Technology will impact every aspect of an organization including the extension of the team concept beyond national geographic boundaries. Technology will facilitate shared leadership and team coordination by enabling supervisors to immediately communicate with other supervisors, joint venture partners, suppliers and outsourcing contractors located in other parts of the world.

Sensitivity Training

Helping employees to feel accepted and appreciated for who they are can be promoted by sensitivity training. Developing empathy with co-workers who are perceived to be different can help all employees to realize that they have more in common with each other than differences. Sensitivity training can also be used to promote the benefits of a diverse workforce and facilitate relationship development and teamwork.

Management of Conflict

Frequent interactions between diverse people can result in disagreements which have the potential to disrupt and impede a company's ability to compete if those disagreements are not properly managed. An additional concern includes the potential for complaints and lawsuits of discrimination to develop, especially when employees from protected groups are involved. Therefore, to facilitate teamwork, understanding and communication, and avoid legal liability, supervisors will need to develop conflict management skills.

Training initiatives will remain a high priority with every organization's strategic planning. At the same time, globalization, technological change and workforce diversity will help ensure the importance of diversity training.

REVIEW QUESTIONS

1. Affirmative action should be discontinued once an organization implements a Diversity Program.

2. What is a Diversity/Cultural Assessment?
3. A Diversity Program is a short-term program.
4. The philosophy organizations should follow, "if it's not broke. . .?"
5. A Diversity Program should primarily focus on the needs of women and minorities.
6. What role should supervisors perform when organizations are implementing change?
7. Why do people resist change?
8. Why is "Managing Diversity" considered to be an organizational change process?
9. What is a major barrier encountered when attempting to implement a Diversity Program?
10. What is a major component of a Diversity Program?

LEARNING ACTIVITIES

1. Divide the class into teams and ask each team to identify what they believe should be the major components for a diversity program.
2. Have a class discussion where students talk about recent diversity related changes that have taken place in the workplace and the impact these changes have had on the employees, management and the organization.

Glossary

Affirmative Action: The government requirement that contractors must undertake extra efforts to actively recruit, hire, and promote qualified women, minorities, persons with disabilities, and Vietnam Era veterans.

Affirmative Action Goals: Refers to hiring targets for women and minorities that contractors promise or commit to achieve by exercising good faith efforts.

Affirmative Action Quotas: Refers to a fixed number or percentage of women or minorities that must be hired for a given job category. Generally, quotas are illegal.

Age Discrimination in Employment Act of 1967 (ADEA): The federal law which prohibits discrimination in employment based on age when a person is age 40 years and older.

Americans with Disabilities Act of 1990 (ADA): The federal law which prohibits employment discrimination against qualified people with protected disabilities.

Applicant evaluation checklist: Refers to a written list (checklist) of job qualifications identified for a given job which can be used to evaluate or compare to the qualifications of each applicant applying for the job.

Assimilation: The Melting Pot theory. When a person gives up his/her ethnic identity and cultural heritage in order to become the stereotyped "ideal" of how a person should be.

At-will employment: An employment relationship where the employer can terminate an employee without notice, at any time, for any reason and without due process.

Baby Boomers: The generation of people born between 1946- 1964.

Change agent: A person responsible for introducing and implementing any change. In most organizations, the supervisors are the principal change agents.

Change Assessment: An assessment used to identify those factors that favor and oppose any given change effort.

Civil Unions: Are similar to marriage licenses for gay couples. They give gay couples most of the rights, protections and benefits of marriage. Only the states of Vermont and Connecticut recognize civil unions.

Defense in Marriage Acts: Over 30 states and the federal government have "Defense in Marriage Acts" which mandate that marriage can only exist between a man and a woman. However, in November of 2003, the Massachusetts's Supreme Court held that the state constitution guarantees gay couples the right to marry. It remains to be seen how many other states will follow Massachusetts and recognize gay marriages (same-sex marriages).

Disability: A mental or physical impairment which substantially limits a major life activity.

Discrimination: Behavior or action based on a prejudicial attitude.

Disparate Impact theory: An employment rule, policy, practice, procedure, or decision that has an unequal or adverse effect on members of a protected group.

Diversity: Refers to the mix of people with various backgrounds, experiences and characteristics. The differences that exist among people based on all characteristics that make one person different from another person, including race, culture, gender, age, physical appearance, religion, disabilities, values, attitudes, ideas, etc.

Diversity (or cultural) assessment: Refers to the process of collecting and analyzing information about a company to evaluate the existing organizational environment or culture.

Diversity Program: A long term plan made up of several components and designed to create an inclusiveness work environment.

Diversity training: A proactive type of training with interrelated short term and long term training components which are designed to address the training needs associated with a diverse workforce. The training modules can be conducted during a single training session or over the course of several sessions.

Documentation: Anything in writing which establishes a record or preserves evidence which can be used to justify or substantiate an employment action or decision.

Equal Employment Opportunity: Refers to the three principal federal antidiscrimination laws (Title VII, ADEA, and ADA) which are designed to prevent employment discrimination based on race, color, religion, national origin, gender, disability and age.

Equal Employment Opportunity Commission (EEOC): The federal agency responsible for enforcing Title VII, the ADEA, and parts of the ADA and EPA.

Equal Pay Act of 1963 (EPA): The federal law which prohibits gender-based wage discrimination. The EPA requires equal pay for men and women performing the same job.

Empowerment: To include employees in organizational decision-making, problem-solving and goal-setting.

Era of economic equality for women: The pre-industrial period of time in American history where the economic contributions of women were at least equal to that of men.

Essential job functions: Refers to the basic or fundamental duties (functions) of a specific job.

Executive Order 11246: Requires affirmative action by federal contractors for women and minorities.

Executive Order 13087: Prohibits employment discrimination against federal employees based on sexual orientation.

Family & Medical Leave Act of 1993: The federal law which allows qualified employees up to 12 weeks of unpaid leave each year for family related or medical emergencies.

Competence training: Refers to training which is designed to help employees develop their job related skills and competency.

Generation X: The generation of people born between 1964–1981.

Generation Y: The generation of people born between 1979–2000.

Globalization: Refers to the world economy or international interactions.

Golden Rule: Treat others as we would like to be treated.

Hostile Work Environment Harassment: A type of (sexual) harassment where an employee is subjected to (a variety of) unwelcome behaviors (of a sexual nature).

Immigration Reform & Control Act of 1986 (IRCA): A federal law which prohibits employment discrimination based on citizenship status or national origin.

Interactive process/dialogue: A meeting between the employer and employee where information is exchanged in an attempt to identify a mutually acceptable accommodation (for a disability or religious belief).

Job description: Identifies the major job functions, such as duties, responsibilities and tasks, to be performed for a particular job.

Job specification: Identifies the qualifications necessary to perform a given job, such as education, skills and work experience.

Learning curve: Refers to the temporary decline in performance that normally occurs when any change is implemented.

Managing diversity: An organizational change process designed to create an inclusive workplace.

Me Principle: The (false) belief that everyone is the same or thinks the same or has the same perceptions as everyone else in the world.

Metrosexual: A term used to describe heterosexual men who have a preference for the latest fashions in clothing and personal appearance, and can freely express their feelings and emotions without embarrassment.

Mind language: Having the same perception or state of mind, as the person we are communicating has in order for words to have the same meanings and for understanding to occur.

Multicultural leadership: Leadership designed to manage a diverse workforce.

Negligent hiring: When an employer fails to exercise reasonable care during the hiring process and as a result a dangerous, incompetent or unqualified person is hired who ends up injuring someone.

New Golden Rule: Treat others as they would like to be treated.

Non-fraternization Policy: A company policy which is designed to regulate or prohibit employee dating.

Office of Federal Contract Compliance Programs (OFCCP): The federal agency responsible for administering affirmative action.

Opportunity cost: The consequence or sacrifice involved when making a choice, where choosing one alternative automatically foregoes another alternative.

Personal comfort zone: Refers to the degree of comfortableness we feel toward a person or group.

Pregnancy Discrimination Act of 1978 (PDA): An amendment to Title VII which is designed to prohibit employment discrimination based on pregnancy, childbirth or related conditions.

Prejudice: An (negative) attitude based on misinformation.

Protected groups: Refers to women, minorities, people with disabilities, and people age 40 years and older.

Qualified person with a disability: A person with a disability who satisfies the job specifications and can perform the essential functions of a job.

Quid Pro Quo Harassment: A type of sexual harassment where an employee is forced to grant sexual favors in exchange for job opportunities, such as a pay raise, promotion, or continued employment.

Reasonable accommodations: Refers to making changes to the workplace or a specific job to enable a qualified person with a disability to perform the essential functions of the job.

Reverse discrimination: Refers to employment discrimination against white males under 40 years old who have no protected disabilities.

Sensitivity training: Training that can create awareness of the feelings and concerns of people, and help them to feel accepted and appreciated for who they are. This type of training can help to develop empathy with co-workers, facilitate relationship development, and promote the benefits of a diverse workforce.

Sex discrimination: Refers to discrimination based on gender. Sex discrimination is a violation of Title VII and means that a person is being treated unfairly because of that person's gender.

Sexual harassment: Refers to a type of employment discrimination based on gender and prohibited by Title VII. There are two types of sexual harassment, Quid Pro Quo and Hostile Work Environment.

Sexual orientation: Refers to our natural sexual predisposition for a person of a given gender. Sexual orientation has replaced the term "sexual preference." No federal law prohibits sexual orientation discrimination in the private employment sector.

Stereotyping: When we assign specific traits to an individual based on his/her physical appearance or perceived membership in a specific group.

Strategic planning: Refers to planning for the future or long term planning.

Tangible employment action: Any employment action or decision that has an economic impact on an employee's job or employment. Examples include, pay, raises, job assignments, continued employment, and promotion.

Title VII of the 1964 Civil Rights Act (Title VII): The federal law which prohibits employment discrimination based on race, color, religion, national origin, and gender.

Transgender: The politically correct term for "transsexual," or a person who believes he/she was born in the wrong body. A person who believes he/she has the mind of one gender and the body of another.

Transvestite: Refers to a person who likes to wear (articles of) the clothing of another gender. Transvestites can be either heterosexual or gay.

Undue hardship: Refers to any job accommodation imposing a significant expense or difficulty on the business.

Values: A set of (permanent) standards or beliefs that a person holds in high regard. Values are a major influence on a person's thinking and behavior.

References

Adler, Nancy J. International Dimensions of Organizational Behavior. Cincinnati, OH.: South-Western College Publishing, 1997.

Bennett-Alexander, Dawn D., and Laura P. Hartman. Employment Law for Business. New York, NY.: McGraw-Hill/Irwin, 2004.

Blank, Renee, and Sandra Slipp. Voices of Diversity. New York, NY.: American Management Association, 1994.

Cox, Taylor. Cultural Diversity in Organizations. San Francisco, CA.: Berrett-Koehler Publishers, Inc., 1993.

Fagenson, Ellen A. Women in Management. Newbury Park, CA.: Sage Publications, Inc., 1993.

Francesco, Anne Marie, and Barry A. Gold. International Organizational Behavior. Upper Saddle River, NJ.: Prentice Hall, 1998.

Gardenswartz, Lee, and Anita Rowe. Managing Diversity: A Complete Desk Reference and Planning Guide. New York, NY.: Business One Irwin/Pfeiffer & Company, 1993.

Gentile, Mary C. Managerial Excellence Through Diversity. Prospect Heights, IL.: Waveland Press, Inc., 1996.

Jackson, Susan E. Diversity in the Workplace. New York, NY.: The Guilford press, 1992.

Koziara, Karen S., Michael H. Moskow, and Lucretia D. Tanner. Working Women: Past, Present, Future. Washington D.C.: The Bureau of National Affairs, 1987.

Reece, Barry L., and Rhonda Brandt. Effective Human Relations: Personal and Organizational Applications. Boston, MA.: Houghton Mifflin Company, 2005.

Thomas, R. Roosevelt. Beyond Race and Gender. New York, NY.: American Management Association, 1991.

Tingley, Judith C. Genderflex: Men & Women Speaking Each Other's Language at Work. New York, NY.: American Management Association, 1994.

About The Author

Ralph Ocon is an Associate Professor of Organizational Leadership and Supervision and the former Equal Employment Opportunity Officer for Purdue University Calumet, located in Hammond, Indiana. A faculty member since 1983, Professor Ocon has taught courses in the areas of diversity management, human behavior, leadership, creative thinking, and human resource and hospitality law. As the Equal Employment Opportunity Officer, from 1990 to 2002, Professor Ocon investigated and resolved complaints of discrimination, conducted diversity related training programs for the university and community, and interacted with local, state and federal governmental agencies responsible for enforcing equal employment opportunity and administering affirmative action.

Professor Ocon has made presentations and published scholarly papers on leadership and diversity management at regional, national and international conferences. In addition to his teaching responsibilities at the university, Professor Ocon is a frequent speaker to community groups and consultant/trainer for businesses throughout Northwest Indiana in the areas of diversity and leadership management.

Professor Ocon has a long association with Purdue University, having received three degrees from Purdue University in West Lafayette, in addition to a law degree from Indiana University in Bloomington, Indiana.

Professor Ocon's educational background, research, consulting, teaching and equal employment opportunity experience provide him with a unique combination of skills and experience in the area of diversity management training and education.